VEGAN VIETNAMESE

Vibrant Plant-Based Recipes to Enjoy Every Day

HELEN LE

Creator of Helen's Recipes

ROCK
POINT

10 9 8 7 6 5 4 3

ISBN: 978-1-63106-930-7

Library of Congress Control Number: 2023933026

Publisher: Rage Kindelsperger
Creative Director: Laura Drew
Senior Art Director: Marisa Kwek
Editorial Director: Erin Canning
Managing Editor: Cara Donaldson
Editor: Amanda Gambill
Cover Design: Marisa Kwek
Interior Design: Lisa Berman
Food Photography: Detas Studio

Printed in the USA

TO ALL VIETNAMESE FOOD FANS
AROUND THE WORLD.

⚭ CONTENTS ⚭

INTRODUCTION

I grew up in Da Nang, Vietnam, but it wasn't until I went abroad to Singapore and Germany for college that I realized how much I loved Vietnamese cuisine. As a result, in 2011, I started my YouTube Channel, *Helen's Recipes*. As it continued to grow, I was given the opportunity not only to revisit my childhood love of cooking, but also to discover a newfound appreciation of my culture and heritage.

After years of posting cooking video tutorials and growing *Helen's Recipes* on YouTube and Facebook, I've realized that many of my subscribers follow a vegan or plant-based diet. I've received countless comments and messages recommending that I make more vegetarian and vegan recipes.

Whether it's due to their beliefs, ethics, or for health or environmental reasons, more and more people are embracing plant-based diets and lifestyles, and Vietnamese cuisine is an excellent fit. Because over 70 percent of the population in Vietnam are either Buddhist or follow Buddhist practices, many are vegetarian. Some even avoid onions and garlic because they believe eating these might increase their libido and drive away good spirits. There are also those who are vegan because of their love of animals and exclude all animal-derived products from their diet. This includes all meats (including fish), as well as dairy products, eggs, and even honey.

Given the diversity in the plant-based community, I always try my best to create recipes that are friendly for all. I've put a lot of effort into completing this book and hope that it will serve as a helpful guide for anyone interested in stepping into the plant-based world via Vietnamese cuisine.

With this book, you'll be able to explore vegan versions of a variety of popular Vietnamese dishes, from the northern, central, and southern regions of the country. My main goal while researching and creating these recipes was for people to be able to enjoy each dish without realizing it is vegan, because it has the same flavor as the traditional version. I also wanted to enrich Vietnamese plant-based cuisine with recipes based on the country's authentic dishes and offer families a wider variety of meal options.

I hope that you enjoy making every recipe in this cookbook. However, before you turn the page and get going, I'd like to thank you again for your support of *Helen's Recipes* and my journey to promote Vietnamese cuisine.

Now, let's get cooking!

THE VIETNAMESE PANTRY

These are some of the most common dried, refrigerated, and fresh ingredients you will find throughout the recipes in this book. If you're unsure about an ingredient and how to prep it, you can always refer to this section. Except where noted, you should be able to find most items at any local or online Asian grocery store.

DRIED AND REFRIGERATED INGREDIENTS

CHAR SIU SEASONING MIX

Char siu seasoning mix has a distinctive red color and adds a unique burst of flavors (both sweet and savory) to your dishes. Although it's intended for seasoning pork, the mix is completely meatless. It's made of sugar, salt, powdered soy sauce, onion and garlic powders, and other spices, including cloves, cinnamon, and star anise. Even the red food coloring is vegan-friendly! Char siu is sold in packs at Asian grocery stores and most large supermarkets. Two of the most popular brands are NOH and Lobo.

DRIED BEAN CURD (TOFU SKIN, YUBA, OR FUZHU)

This ingredient normally comes in sticks or sheets. You should be able to find it in the refrigerated

section of your local grocery store or the dried foods section of any Asian grocery store. To prepare it for cooking, soak it in room-temperature water forabout 20 minutes to let it soften, and then drain. You can then add it to salads, hot pots, stews, or briefly deep-fry it for a crispy snack.

DRIED MOCK BEEF SLICES

Dried mock or vegan beef slices are dehydrated, textured vegetable and soy protein. They're sold in packs at most Asian grocery stores, but they're also available online. This vegan beef substitute can transform any plant-based recipe into a textured, savory meal. Before incorporating the slices, just soak them in water for 15 minutes to rehydrate them, squeeze out the excess water, and then cook according to the recipe instructions.

FERMENTED SOYBEAN SAUCE

Made from fermented glutinous rice, soybeans, sea salt, and water, fermented soybean sauce ranges in color from brown to dark brown. It tastes much more like Japanese miso than soy sauce. In Vietnam, this sauce is mainly used for dipping foods, including fresh spring rolls (page 53), but it can also be used to season braised dishes. Some of the most famous tương is tương Bần from the Bần village in Hưng Yên Province and tương Cự Đà from the Cự Đà village in Hanoi. However, many people use tương and tương Bần interchangeably when referring to fermented soybean sauce. You might also encounter tương hột, which is made from whole-grain boiled soybeans mixed with ground-roasted soybeans, and fermented by rice or corn mold.

FRIED TOFU

You can buy fried tofu at most Asian or organic grocery stores, which can be a real time-saver if you don't want to fry your own. It comes in precut blocks, and you can usually find it in the refrigerated produce section.

MUNG BEANS

Peeled split mung beans are available in plastic bags at most Asian grocery stores. After you cook them, you can mash them into a paste by hand or in a food processor, or you can freeze them to use later. Here's how to make mashed mung beans:

1 cup (200 g) peeled split mung beans

1 cup (240 ml) water

1. Place beans in a mesh strainer, rinse thoroughly to remove any dirt, and then transfer to a large bowl.

2. Add water until it is at least 2 inches (5 cm) over top of beans. Let soak for at least 1 hour or overnight, and then drain.

3. Combine 1 cup (240 ml) of water and mung beans in a large saucepan with a tight-fitting lid. Bring to a boil and cook uncovered over medium heat until water level drops below surface of beans (about 5 minutes).

4. Reduce heat to low and cover, leaving lid slightly askew to allow steam to escape and prevent contents from boiling over. Let simmer for 15 minutes.

5. Remove from heat and let sit until beans have a soft and creamy—but not grainy—texture (about 5 minutes). Allow to cool.

NOODLES

Most Vietnamese noodles are made from rice and tapioca starch. They come in various sizes, shapes, and textures, including flat rice (bánh phở), thin and round slippery rice vermicelli (bún), translucent and thin glass (miến), yellow turmeric flat rice (mì Quảng), translucent and chewy rice (hủ tiếu dai), and so on.

Most also come in dried form, which you either can cook following package directions or following these quick instructions. Vinegar helps the noodles retain their shape, while the vegetable oil prevents them from sticking. To reduce the cook time, you can soak your noodles in water for 5 to 10 minutes before boiling. The final step will also prevent the noodles from forming into a solid block, making it easier to fluff and separate them.

10 cups (2.4 L) water

1 tablespoon vinegar

1 teaspoon vegetable oil

16 ounces (454 g) dried noodles (bánh phở, bún, hủ tiếu dai, or mì Quảng)

1. Pour water in a large saucepan, bring to a boil, and then add vinegar and vegetable oil.

2. Add dried noodles and boil until al dente (5 to 10 minutes).

3. Remove from heat, drain, and rinse under cold water to remove excess starch and stop cooking process.

4. Rinse again with hot water to help noodles dry out faster and reduce clumping.

5. Place a bowl facedown in a strainer, and then drain noodles over it.

RICE PAPER WRAPPERS

Vietnamese spring rolls are wrapped in rice paper. The most common are bánh đa nem in the North and bánh tráng lề, which is a no-soak type from Central Vietnam. Because the no-soak wrappers aren't fully dried, mold will form on them if they're not used fairly quickly. As a result, few Asian grocery stores outside of Vietnam can carry them. Luckily, you can substitute Chinese spring roll pastry wrappers or normal Vietnamese rice paper.

To soften Vietnamese rice paper, add 1 tablespoon each of sugar and lime juice, and 2 cups (480 ml) of water to a bowl. Don't just dip the wrappers in the water, though—that will make them too wet. Instead, wet your fingers in the bowl, and then spread liquid over the surface of one side of the rice paper. This will help your rolls get as golden brown and crispy as possible. Place the wrapper on a flat surface and add 1 tablespoon of filling closer to one end. Lift up that end, fold it, push it back a little bit, and then fold in both sides. Continue to roll tightly all the way to the other end.

SEITAN (WHEAT GLUTEN)

Seitan (also called wheat protein or wheat gluten) has a chewy, stringy texture that resembles meat, so it is often used as an alternative in Asian vegetarian, Buddhist, and macrobiotic dishes. In Vietnam, seitan comes in a tube shape, about the size of a sausage. You can buy Vietnamese-style seitan in a can or frozen at most Asian grocery stores or online. However, if you want to make your own, you will need vital wheat gluten, which can be found at most large supermarkets (I use Bob's Red Mill Textured Vital Wheat Gluten). However, do note that it could appear darker in color (more of a yellow-brown) depending on the brand.

If you want to make seitan that is exactly the same shape and form as that found in Vietnam, you'll need to purchase five 5 by 1-inch (12.5 by 2.5 cm) cannoli (a.k.a. cream horn) molds. You can find these at most big-box stores or order them online. Otherwise, you can simply cut seitan into bite-size slices for use in most recipes.

½ cup plus 2 tablespoons (150 ml) lukewarm (104°F/40°C) water

⅛ teaspoon baking powder

⅛ teaspoon salt

¾ cup (96 g) vital wheat gluten, sifted

1. In a medium bowl, combine lukewarm water, baking powder, and salt, and stir until solids are dissolved. Add wheat gluten and mix well with a rubber spatula.

2. Knead the dough gently for 1 to 2 minutes, and then transfer to a 4 by 4-inch (10 by 10 cm) container. Cover with plastic wrap and let sit for 1 hour.

3. Cut dough into five ½-inch (1 cm) thick slices, and then, starting slightly above one end, wrap and twist each slice around a cannoli mold. Pinch the bottom end of the dough together to close it. Alternatively, you can cut each slice of dough into bite-size pieces.

4. Bring a large pot of water to a boil, drop in the bite-size pieces or molds of dough, and boil until they float to the top (about 3 minutes).

5. Transfer to a large bowl of cold water, let cool for a few minutes, and then push to release seitan from molds or drain any remaining water from bite-size pieces.

SESAME RICE CRACKERS

As the name implies, Vietnamese sesame rice crackers (bánh tráng mè or bánh đa vừng) are made from rice and sesame seeds. They normally come in packs of dried rounds and are available at most Asian grocery stores. To prepare them, you can grill the dried crackers on a charcoal grill or infrared stove. Flip them occasionally until they're puffy and crispy on both sides. You can also cook them in the microwave on high for 1 minute on both sides.

SHIITAKE MUSHROOMS

Most often associated with Japanese cuisine, shiitake mushrooms are also native to Korea and regions in eastern China, where they grow on decaying logs and trees. They add a smoky flavor to any dish, but they are particularly ideal for adding a meaty texture to vegan and vegetarian dishes. While you can find fresh shiitake mushrooms at many grocery stores, they are sold more widely in dried form, which should always be rehydrated before cooking.

To do so, just submerge the mushrooms in a bowl of room-temperature or warm water and soak until they double in size (about 20 minutes). Then, drain, remove the stems, and cut or slice them to your desired shape.

SOY SAUCE

An essential condiment in Asian cuisine, soy sauce is made from fermented soybeans. It packs a powerful flavor punch that is simultaneously salty and sweet with just a hint of bitterness. You should have no trouble finding soy sauce at any grocery store. However, it is important to note that wheat flour is used in the fermenting process, so those with a gluten sensitivity will want to look for a gluten-free brand. Also, some manufacturers add non-vegan flavor enhancers, including some that come from fish and meat, so make sure to read the ingredients.

STICKY RICE

Also known as glutinous (although it doesn't contain any gluten) or sweet rice, sticky rice is high in amylopectin starch and low in amylose starch. When cooked, the grains develop a glue-like texture and stick together in a mass. In Vietnam, the short-grain, opaque white sticky rice is the most popular, but if it's not available in your area, you can use the long-grain Thai/Lao varieties as well.

The best way to cook this dish is to steam it because the grains will stay relatively whole and separate. The rice will need to be rinsed, soaked for 4 to 8 hours, and drained before steaming. The best steamers for sticky rice are bamboo or tiered metal. Just line the steamer basket with a piece of banana leaf or parchment paper to prevent any rice from falling through the grates and sticking. Wrap the steamer lid in a large kitchen towel and tie the corners of the fabric over the handle. This will absorb the excess steam and prevent it from dropping back into the rice.

While you can cook sticky rice on a stovetop or in a rice cooker, the grains will come out quite disintegrated and meld into big sticky lumps. If you cook it this way, it's always a good idea to grease a ladle or chopsticks (or simply dip them in water) before fluffing and dividing the rice to prevent it from sticking.

1. COOK STICKY RICE ON A STOVETOP Soak the rice in water for 1 hour, and then drain.

2. Cover the bottom of a pot that has a tight-fitting lid evenly with the rice. Do not fill the pot more than halfway as the rice needs a lot of steam to cook and room to expand. Add just enough liquid (water, coconut milk, bean cooking water, and so on) to barely cover the rice. Bring to a boil and cook uncovered over medium heat until the water is mostly evaporated (about 10 minutes). Reduce the heat to low, cover the pot with the lid, and let it simmer for 15 more minutes.

3. Remove from heat and let it sit until rice is somewhat translucent, without any white in the grains (about 5 minutes).

1. COOK STICKY RICE IN A RICE COOKER Soak the rice in water for 1 hour, and then drain. Fill the rice cooker a bit less than halfway with the sticky rice until it covers the bottom evenly. Add just enough liquid (water, coconut milk, bean cooking water, and so on) to barely cover the rice, and then press Cook or Start.

2. When the appliance beeps to signify it is finished cooking, let it sit for an additional 5 minutes and do not remove the lid.

TOFU

Also known as bean curd, tofu is essentially curdled soy milk cut into squares. It is used in many vegan and vegetarian dishes because it easily absorbs the flavors of other ingredients, while also adding texture. It is available at any grocery store in the produce section and comes in five different textures: silken (which is the softest), regular, firm, extra-firm, and super-firm. Firm is the texture called for in most recipes. Before cooking tofu, simply remove it from the package and pat it dry with a clean kitchen towel.

VEGETABLE OR MUSHROOM STOCK POWDER (MUSHROOM SEASONING GRANULE)

Most Vietnamese people season vegetarian and vegan dishes with mushroom seasoning granule (hạt nêm chay) to add an umami (meaty or savory) flavor. Mushroom seasoning granule can include iodine salt, flavor enhancers, tapioca starch, vegetable oil, mushroom flavor and powder, and synthetic vegetable flavor. Some of the most popular brands in Vietnam are Knorr, Maggi, and Aji-ngon. You can also substitute vegetable or mushroom stock powder.

VEGETARIAN OYSTER SAUCE

Oyster sauce is a condiment called for in many Asian dishes to add a jolt of savory, tangy (and fishy) flavor. Because it is made with oyster extracts, you will want to use a vegetarian or vegan version, such as Wan Ja Shan or Lee Kum Kee, both of which are available at most grocery stores.

WOOD EAR MUSHROOMS

Wood ear mushrooms grow on the bark of elder trees and look like ears, hence their name. Earthy and mild in flavor, they're popular in Chinese and Vietnamese cooking due to their crunchy texture and ability to easily absorb seasonings. Often sold in dried form, they (and any other dried mushrooms) should always be rehydrated before cooking. To do so, just submerge them in a bowl of warm or room-temperature water. Let them soak until they become soft and pliable and expand to three or four times their original size (about 15 minutes). Then, trim off the roots and cut them into the desired shape.

FRESH INGREDIENTS

ASIAN BASIL

Also known as Thai basil, this herb is native to Southeast Asia and adds a spicy, licorice-like flavor. It's green and leafy just like regular sweet basil, but has a purple stem. You should be able to find it at most Asian grocery stores, but you can also substitute regular sweet basil, along with some cilantro and mint to mimic the flavor.

ASIAN DWARF BANANAS

For the banana desserts in this collection, you'll want to use Asian dwarf bananas, which are also known as pisang awak and dwarf nam wah. In Vietnamese, they're called chuối xiêm or chuối sứ. They're chubbier and shorter than Western bananas and have a more golden skin when ripe. Outside of Vietnam, you should be able to find peeled, frozen packs of Asian dwarf bananas at most Asian grocery stores.

ASIAN SHALLOTS

Also called Thai shallots, these small, bulbous, reddish alliums add a mild sweet flavor to any dish. Although you can order them fresh online, Asian shallots are difficult to find fresh in the US. In a pinch, you can substitute with regular shallots.

BANANA BLOSSOMS

Also known as banana flower or banana heart, banana blossom is a purple, tear-shaped flower that grows at the end of a banana fruit cluster. The inner yellowish, tightly packed petals are more tender and edible than the outer, darker petals. It is traditionally used in Vietnamese salads or soups. However, it does not taste like banana; its flavor is milder and more similar to artichoke. If you cannot find fresh banana blossom, you can substitute 1 part red cabbage to 4 parts white cabbage, finely shredded.

Here's how to prep banana blossom:

1 tablespoon vinegar

4 cups (1 L) cold water

1 medium-trunk (about 18 ounces/510 g)
banana blossom

1. Combine vinegar and water in a large bowl.

2. Remove and discard the thick outer layers of banana
blossoms and any flowers in between. With a sharp knife
or mandoline, slice banana blossoms crosswise into
very thin rings and place in bowl immediately to prevent
discoloring. Let sit for 10 to 15 minutes.

3. Rinse thoroughly under cold water and drain.

BANANA LEAVES

As you might have guessed, banana leaves are leaves
from a banana tree. While inedible, they are used for
both display and as a wrap to add a mild, yet earthy,
flavor to many Asian dishes. Banana leaves are widely
available, but if you can't find them at the supermarket,
check your local Asian grocery store. Before you use
banana leaves, tear them into the desired size, then
blanch them in boiling water for about 30 seconds
to sterilize them. Remove them from the water, set on
a flat surface, and wipe them dry with a kitchen towel.
Let them cool completely before using.

BIRD'S EYE CHILI PEPPERS

These small, pointed peppers are green when unripe
and red when mature. Both are used often in Asian
cuisines to add a bitter (green) or fruity and sweet
(red) flavor. The main thing to remember is both colors
are about twenty-two times hotter than a jalapeño,
so it's a good idea to wear gloves whenever you are
working with them. Also, when using in sliced form,
always slice them on the bias. You should be able to
find these chili peppers year-round at the supermarket
or your local Asian grocery store.

CILANTRO (CORIANDER)

This herb is comprised of the green leaves and stalks
of the coriander plant. It is used in many Asian dishes
to add a fresh, yet citrusy flavor. You can buy it fresh
in the produce section of any grocery store. However,
Vietnamese coriander (rau răm), which is also
called Vietnamese mint, is different. It has oblong,
pointed, flat leaves with a purple streak mid-leaf
and tastes lemony and peppery.

ENOKI MUSHROOMS

Enoki (or golden needle) mushrooms are long, thin,
and white, and sold in clusters. The interconnected roots
at the base should always be trimmed off before cooking.
They have a mild flavor and crunchy texture. They are
also highly nutritious and contain a good amount of
fiber, antioxidants, and B vitamins.

GINGER

This tropical flowering plant is native to Southeast Asia,
but it is the root that is used to add a spicy zing to any
dish. You can buy fresh ginger root in the produce section
of any grocery store. You don't have to peel it, but if you
want to, using a potato peeler will make the job much
easier. Then, just slice, grind, or mince it as desired.
In a pinch, you can also use ginger powder, which is
available in the spice aisle of any grocery store.

GREEN CHILI PEPPERS

There are many different varieties of green chili peppers,
but for the recipes in this book, you will be using unripe
bird's eye, jalapeño, or serrano chili peppers. Because
green peppers are unripened, they add a spicy, yet bitter
flavor to the dishes to which they are added. You can find
them in the produce section of your local supermarket
or at an Asian grocery store.

JACKFRUIT

Jackfruit is a large, heavy tropical fruit with a thick,
bumpy rind. It is prevalent in both North and South
Vietnam. When ripe, people eat the sweet, stringy
golden pulp. Young, unripe green jackfruit has a meatier
texture that absorbs spices very well, so it can be used
in a variety of dishes. In the United States, it's widely
used as a pork substitute, particularly in pulled "pork"
sandwiches. Unfortunately, fresh jackfruit isn't available
outside of the areas in which it grows natively; however,
you can buy canned young jackfruit in brine at most
Asian grocery stores. You can also substitute breadfruit
for green jackfruit, as it has a similar appearance
and texture.

LEEKS

Along with onions and garlic, leeks are part of the allium family, but Vietnamese Buddhists often substitute them for other alliums in their vegetarian dishes. This is why you'll see leek called for in many of these recipes. However, if you prefer onions, scallions, or garlic, feel free to use those instead. Leeks can be nearly 20 inches (50 cm) long with a round, thick white end. The leaves are solid, flat, and folded like garlic leaves. The dark-green leafy part is edible, but quite hard. I remove the green parts and use only the bulb (the white part near the root and the soft, light-green part at the core). Rinse leeks well, drain, and pat them dry. You can then slice or mince them, and marinate before adding them to fried or stir-fried dishes.

LEMONGRASS

This tropical grass is native to parts of Asia, Africa, and Australia. The stalks are used in many Asian dishes to add a zesty lemon flavor, hence the name. You can buy lemongrass fresh in the produce section of any grocery store, but it also comes in dried or powdered form, which you can find in the spice aisle. If adding the stalks to flavor a dish, you need to prep them. First, trim off the green upper parts and lowest, toughest portions at the bases of the stalks. Then, place them on a cutting board and bruise the bulbous end with a pestle or meat tenderizer to release fragrance and flavor.

LIME LEAVES

As the name implies, limes leaves come from lime trees. Makrut lime leaves are used in many Asian dishes to add a slightly bitter tartness and citrusy aromatic scent. You can buy them fresh, frozen, or dried at most Asian grocery stores.

LIMES

You will find these small, green citrus fruits in the produce section of any grocery store. Many Asian dishes are served with lime wedges so diners can squeeze the fresh juice over their meal before eating.

MINT

The leaves of the mint plant are used in many Asian dishes, but their cool, sweet flavor is often particularly associated with Vietnamese cuisine. You can find fresh mint leaves in the produce section of any grocery store, and most recipes in this book call for them to be roughly chopped. However, Vietnamese mint (rau răm), which is also called Vietnamese coriander, is different. It has oblong, pointed, flat leaves with a purple streak mid-leaf and tastes lemony and peppery.

MUNG BEAN SPROUTS

These are the thin, white stalks that grow out of mung beans, and they are regularly used in many Asian cuisines. They have a delicate flavor that is similar to green peas and you can find them in the produce section of any grocery store.

MUSTARD GREENS

There are many varieties of mustard greens (Brassica jucea) that differ greatly in heat, flavor, and appearance. For most recipes in this book, you can use cải cay (Vietnamese) or juk gai choy (Cantonese), which is a leafy, light green romaine with a narrow, celery-shaped stem. It has a remarkable peppery taste with just a hint of mustard. You can also substitute leafy, soft lettuce leaves, such as Batavia, green leaf lettuce, or kale.

However, the kind that makes the best pickles is cải bẹ dưa or cải sen (mature, large gai choy in Chinese). These look like loose-headed Chinese cabbage, with very thick stems and bases. They have a pungent, peppery, horseradish-like flavor and are curved with crinkled, matte, bright green leaves. Choose those with large stems if you enjoy the crunchier parts of pickles and leave them near a window in the sunlight or just out on the kitchen counter for a day to wilt before pickling. You never want to immediately pickle anything you've just taken out of the refrigerator—unless you like soggy pickles.

You can find mustard greens in the fresh produce section of most Asian grocery stores. To prep them, just rinse them well and remove the stems.

PANDAN LEAVES

Known as the "vanilla of the East," pandan leaves are commonly used as a sweet flavoring agent in Southeast Asian cuisines. You can buy them fresh or frozen at most Asian grocery stores.

To use them, tie a few in a knot and drop them into any dish (such as sticky rice, coconut sauce, and so on) as it cooks, and then simply remove and discard them. You can also use them as a natural source of green food coloring. To do so, finely chop about 10 leaves for every 1 cup (240 ml) of water, and combine in a food processor until smooth. Then, strain to separate the leaves.

PERILLA LEAVES

Perilla is a species in the mint family that grows natively in Southeast Asia and India. Its leaves are purple and green on both sides and when used in food, they add a unique minty-basil flavor with just a hint of cumin. You should be able to find perilla leaves in the produce section at your local supermarket or Asian grocery store.

SCALLIONS

Part of the allium family, scallions are also called green or spring onions. They have a white base and long green stalks, both of which are used in many Asian recipes. The white part tastes like a milder version of a regular white onion, while the green stalks add a hint of grassiness. You can find them in the produce section of any grocery store.

TAMARIND

You can usually find tamarind pulp, or dried tamarind in 1-pound (454 g) blocks at an Asian grocery store. To prepare for cooking, just break the block into smaller pieces, and then soak them in hot water. To create a tamarind paste, you can mash the pulp, press it through a strainer, and then discard the fibrous part. You can also buy tamarind paste or concentrate in ready-to-use jars at most Asian or Hispanic grocery stores. However, you might need to add a bit more than the recipe calls for to ensure the flavor will be strong enough. When it comes to sourness, not all tamarind pulps and pastes are created equal. You might have to adjust the tamarind or sugar amounts in certain recipes to get a well-balanced sweet-and-sour flavor. Failing all of the above options, you can also substitute 2 tablespoons (30 ml) of lime juice and 1 tablespoon of brown sugar.

TARO

Taro (Colocasia esculenta) is a starchy, tropical root vegetable widely used in Asian cuisines. There are two basic types: a small, round variety with hairy skin and white/ivory flesh, and a larger, longer type with coarse, outer skin and purple-tinged flesh. All the recipes in this book call for the latter variety. Due to the calcium oxalate it contains, handling taro can make your skin very itchy, so make sure you always wear gloves when peeling or cutting this tuber. It also must be fully cooked before eating to prevent itchy throat or mouth.

SAUCES, CONDIMENTS & PICKLES

When it comes to just about any Vietnamese dish, it's all about the sauces and condiments. From the ever-popular chili jam to a vegan version of fish sauce, this section covers it all. When you make your own sauces and condiments, it gives you complete control over all the ingredients, and once you get the processes down, you'll have the base for lots of dishes. You will also learn how to pickle some staple Vietnamese ingredients, including mustard greens and daikon, so they will be at your fingertips and ready to go whenever you are.

VEGAN FISH SAUCE

Many vegans and vegetarians often replace fish sauce (nước mắm) with a vegan soy sauce, but this substitution can change the look of a dish and lack that savory flavor. I tested many vegan versions and found that the following recipe tastes the best. It yields a salty, briny liquid with a deep umami flavor. The seaweed also provides a hint of "fish" for your taste buds. You can flavor any vegan or vegetarian dish with this sauce, or use it to make the dipping sauce below.

SKILL LEVEL Moderate | **YIELD** 11 ounces (325 ml)

½ ounce (14 g) dried shiitake mushrooms

1 sheet (4 by 8 inches/10 by 20 cm) dried kelp (kombu seaweed)

2½ cups (600 ml) water

7 ounces (200 g) pineapple, peeled and thinly sliced

2 ounces (50 g) salt

2 ounces (50 g) rock sugar

1 cinnamon stick

1 star anise

½ teaspoon soy sauce

1. In a medium saucepan, combine dried shiitake mushrooms, dried kelp, and water, and bring to a boil over medium heat.

2. Boil for 5 minutes, and then add pineapple, salt, rock sugar, cinnamon, star anise, and soy sauce.

3. Simmer on low heat until the sauce is reduced by half, about 30 minutes.

4. Strain to remove all solids, let cool, and then transfer to an airtight glass jar or bottle.

5. Store in the refrigerator for up to 1 month.

VEGAN FISH DIPPING SAUCE

SKILL LEVEL Basic | **YIELD** 3½ ounces (100 ml)

2 tablespoons vegan fish sauce (above)

1 tablespoon sugar

¼ cup (60 ml) water

2 teaspoons lime juice

1 teaspoon garlic, minced

1 teaspoon bird's eye chili pepper, minced

1. In a small bowl, combine vegan fish sauce, sugar, water, and lime juice, and stir well until sugar is completely dissolved.

2. Add garlic and chili pepper to float on top.

HOMEMADE CHAO

Chao, or fermented bean curd, is a popular ingredient in the central and southern regions of Vietnam and is widely used in many plant-based dishes. While the smell is quite strong, once you acquire a taste for it, this condiment can be quite addictive! Chao can be mashed and used to make marinades or a dipping sauce (page 23), but like other fermented foods, such as pickles or yogurt, it requires some experience to make correctly. Many factors, like the weather and the temperature of the room in which you store it, can all affect it, so make sure to read through this recipe before you begin.

SKILL LEVEL Advanced | **YIELD** 4 (6-ounce/177-ml) glass jars

TOFU

3 cups (720 ml) water

1 tablespoon salt

1 block (14 ounces/400 g) firm tofu

1 tablespoon salt and pepper mix (1 part freshly ground black pepper to 12 parts kosher salt) or chili powder

BRINE

3 cups (720 ml) water

1¾ ounces (50 g) salt

½ ounce (15 g) sugar

½ cup (120 ml) Chinese rice wine

1. PREPARE THE TOFU In a medium saucepan, combine water and salt and bring to a boil over high heat. Gently drop in block of tofu and cook over medium-low heat for about 3 minutes to sterilize it.

2. Remove pan from heat and, using a slotted spoon, carefully transfer tofu to a clean kitchen towel. Wrap tofu in towel and place something reasonably heavy (a serving plate, cutting board, soup cans, etc.) on top to squeeze out as much moisture as possible. Let sit for 10 minutes. (You can also place tofu on a pair of crossed chopsticks on a plate and microwave for 30 seconds to remove excess water. This will also sterilize it and give it a firmer texture, making it easier to ferment). Cut tofu block into 1-inch (2.5 cm) cubes.

3. Line a glass tray with a clean kitchen towel and arrange tofu cubes on it about ½ inch (1 cm) apart. Cover with a paper towel, and then cover everything with plastic wrap or cheesecloth to protect it from air and insects.

4. Leave the tray next to a window for 3 to 5 days, until a yellow or brown coating forms on the surface of the tofu (if you live in a hot climate, the tofu will ferment faster).

5. Lift the tofu cubes gently with a rubber spatula or chopsticks (they'll be quite soft and delicate, about the consistency of cream cheese). Roll each cube in salt and pepper mixture (or chili powder if you prefer it to be a bit spicier), and then place in four 6-ounce (180 ml) sterilized glass jars (page 34).

6. MAKE THE BRINE Combine water, salt, and sugar in a small saucepan over medium heat and stir well until salt and sugar are dissolved. When it comes to a boil, remove from heat and allow to cool completely.

7. Gently pour brine into each jar until it covers tofu cubes, and then add 2 tablespoons of Chinese rice wine to each jar. Tightly close the lids and leave undisturbed at room temperature—between 70° and 79° F (22° and 26° C)—for about 5 days (leave for 10 days if you live in a colder climate).

8. When tofu consistency is rich and creamy, it's done! Store in the refrigerator for up to 3 months.

CHAO DIPPING SAUCE

SKILL LEVEL Basic | **YIELD** ¼ cup (60 ml)

2 cubes store-bought or homemade chao (page 22), finely mashed

1 large clove garlic, finely crushed

1 bird's eye chili pepper, finely minced

1 tablespoon sugar

1 tablespoon kumquat or lime juice

In a small bowl, combine the mashed chao, garlic, chili pepper, sugar, and kumquat juice, and mix well until sugar is dissolved.

CHILI JAM

When you visit a restaurant in Central Vietnam, you'll see a jar of chili jam (tương ớt sa tế) on the table. Many visitors to the country have fallen in love with it and asked me how to make it. This condiment is sweet and slightly spicy, but it is especially delicious with noodle dishes. You can use any kind of red chili pepper you prefer, just remember to consider the level of spiciness and your tolerance. You can replace some of the tomatoes with more chili peppers to increase the spiciness.

SKILL LEVEL Advanced | **YIELD** 1 (13½-ounce/400-ml) glass jar

10½ ounces (300 g) red chili peppers

7 ounces (200 g) plum tomatoes

½ cup (120 ml) water

3 tablespoons vegetable oil

1 head garlic, minced

4 shallots, thinly sliced

½ cup (100 g) sugar

1½ teaspoons kosher salt

¼ cup (32 g) toasted sesame seeds

1. With a sharp knife, make a slash lengthwise along each chili pepper.

2. Fill a large saucepan halfway with water and bring to a boil over high heat. Blanch the chili peppers and tomatoes in boiling water for 2 to 3 minutes, and then transfer to an ice-water bath (this halts the cooking process). When completely cool, remove from water and pat dry.

3. Peel tomatoes, remove the seeds, and cut into small chunks. While wearing gloves (particularly if you have sensitive skin), remove seeds from chili peppers and cut them into small pieces.

4. Place tomatoes, chili pepper pieces, and ½ cup (120 ml) of water in a blender or food processor and pulse until smooth.

5. Heat oil in a large skillet over medium-low heat until bubbles appear around a submerged chopstick (about 2 minutes). Add garlic and shallots, and cook and stir until golden brown (about 45 seconds). Stir in chili-tomato purée, sugar, and salt. Bring to a boil, and then reduce heat to medium-low and simmer, stirring and scraping down sides occasionally, until thickened to the consistency of jam (30 to 40 minutes). Stir in sesame seeds and remove from heat.

6. Let jam cool completely, and then store in an airtight 13½-ounce (400 ml) jar in the refrigerator.

7. Store in the refrigerator for up to 1 month. If you cover it with a thin layer of vegetable oil, it will keep for up to 3 months.

SCALLION OIL

Scallion oil (mỡ hành) is a simple garnish used on many Vietnamese dishes, but especially those that are grilled. It adds a pleasant aroma and richness, and its vibrant green color enhances presentation, as well. I recommend using a neutral-flavored oil, like vegetable or canola, to highlight the aroma of these green onions.

SKILL LEVEL Basic | **YIELD** ¼ cup (60 ml)

½ cup (80 g) finely chopped scallions (green parts only)

¼ teaspoon salt

¼ teaspoon sugar

¼ cup (60 ml) vegetable oil

1. In a small, heatproof bowl, combine scallions, salt, and sugar.

2. In a small skillet cook oil over medium heat. When it starts to smoke, immediately remove from heat, pour over the scallions, and stir well. Alternatively, you can combine the scallions, salt, sugar, and oil in a small microwave-safe bowl and heat it on high for 15 seconds. Then, remove and stir well.

3. Store in an airtight glass container in the refrigerator for up to 1 week.

ANNATTO OIL

Annatto oil (dầu màu điều) is a natural food coloring made from annatto seeds. You should be able to find it in most Asian stores, or you can order it online. It's flavorless, but will add the perfect shade of vibrant orange to your favorite Vietnamese dishes.

SKILL LEVEL Basic | **YIELD** ¼ cup (60 ml)

¼ cup (60 ml) vegetable oil

1 tablespoon annatto seeds

1. Heat vegetable oil in a small pan over medium-low heat. When hot, add annatto seeds and fry until oil is vibrant orange (about 2 to 3 minutes). Remove from heat and let cool for 15 to 20 minutes to get a deeper orange.

2. Strain oil through a fine-mesh sieve and discard seeds.

3. Store in an airtight glass container at room temperature for up to 1 week or in the refrigerator for up to 2 weeks.

PICKLED MIXED VEGETABLES

You can customize the vegetables in this recipe (rau củ muối chua) to your taste. For more diverse and colorful pickle jars, try adding shallots, daikon, kohlrabi, jalapeños, bell peppers, or any other vibrant veggies. As the water content used for each kind of vegetable is different, pickling with acid has a lower margin for error because it's a quicker process.

SKILL LEVEL Moderate	YIELD 2 (47-ounce/1.4-L) glass jars

BRINE

3 cups (705 ml) white distilled vinegar

1½ cups (200 g) sugar

3 cups (705 ml) water

VEGETABLES

1 medium head cauliflower (about 1⅓ pounds/600 g), cut into bite-size florets

2 medium carrots, peeled and cut into flower-shaped slices (see Note)

2 medium cucumbers, halved, seeds removed, and cut into ¼- to ½-inch (0.6 to 1 cm) thick slices

1 teaspoon salt

5 large cloves garlic, green cores removed and thinly sliced lengthwise

3 bird's eye or cayenne chili peppers, sliced or whole

1. MAKE THE BRINE In a large pourable jug, combine all ingredients for the brine and stir until solids are dissolved.

2. PREP AND PACK THE VEGETABLES In a large bowl, combine cauliflower, carrots, cucumber, and salt. Toss well and let sit until moisture is drawn out of vegetables (about 30 minutes).

3. Rinse with cold water two or three times to remove excess salt, and then drain thoroughly.

4. Arrange vegetables, garlic, and chili peppers in two 47-ounce (1.4 L) sterilized glass jars (page 34), and then cover with brine. Use two bamboo skewers to press the vegetables into the brine. Close the lid tightly and store in a cool, dry place. After 1 to 2 days, they will be ready to eat.

5. Store in the refrigerator for up to 1 month. (If the pickles start to turn too sour while storing them, simply drain all the liquid and store in an airtight container or a fresh glass jar in the refrigerator.)

 NOTE *To cut a carrot into flower-shaped slices, peel it, and then cut it crosswise into manageable lengths (about 4 inches/10 cm). Next, cut 5 evenly spaced, shallow, V-shaped grooves around the carrot using the knife blade. Finally, place the carrot horizontally on your cutting board and cut it into thin slices.*

PICKLED MUSTARD GREENS

Pickled mustard greens (dưa cải chua) offer just the right amount of crunch and tartness to perfectly pair with almost any rich or savory dish. There are so many things you can add them to as well, including stews, stir-fries, soups, and curries. However, you can also enjoy them on their own as a snack or use them to complement any braised dish.

SKILL LEVEL Advanced | **YIELD** 2 (47-ounce/1.4-L) glass jars

BRINE

6 cups (1.5 L) water

1½ tablespoons salt

1 tablespoon sugar

½ cup (120 ml) rice rinse water

VEGETABLES

2 pounds (907 g) fresh mustard greens (cải bẹ or gai choy), wilted (page 16) and stems removed

2 ounces (56 g) shallots, thinly sliced

3½ ounces (100 g) scallions, cut into 3-inch (7.5 cm) lengths

3 bird's eye chili peppers

1. MAKE THE BRINE In a large saucepan, combine all ingredients except the rice water, and bring to a boil over high heat. Once salt and sugar are dissolved, remove from heat and let cool.

2. Stir in the rice water and then pour into jars with the vegetables you want to pickle. Trim any bruised, yellow, or blemished sections off the mustard greens. Cut into 2-inch (5 cm) lengths and rinse well.

3. PREP AND PACK THE VEGETABLES Trim any bruised, yellow, or blemished sections off the mustard greens. Cut into 2-inch (5 cm) lengths and rinse well.

4. Fill a medium saucepan halfway with water, bring to a boil, and then remove from heat.

5. When the water is no longer bubbling, stir in the mustard greens, making sure they are fully submerged. (You can place a small plate directly on top of them to weigh them down, if necessary. Just make sure it doesn't fully cover the pot so that steam can escape.) Let sit for at least 4 hours or overnight. After the water cools, you can cover the pan to prevent contamination.

6. After soaking, the mustard greens should be light yellow and have a strong mustard smell. Drain and squeeze them dry. Empty the water from the saucepan, and then place the mustard greens back in it. Add the shallots and scallions, and toss well.

7. Pack the mustard greens mixture and chili peppers into two 47-ounce (1.4 L) sterilized glass jars (page 34), and then pour in enough brine to completely cover them. Use two bamboo skewers to press the vegetables into the brine. Close the lid tightly and leave the jar undisturbed on the kitchen counter for 3 days.

8. After the allotted time, taste a mustard green; if sour, they are ready to serve, but if not, continue to ferment for up to 2 more days.

9. To stop the fermentation process, simply drain all the pickling liquid. You can then store your pickled mustard greens in an airtight container or a fresh glass jar in the refrigerator for up to 1 month.

PICKLED CARROTS AND DAIKON

Pickled carrots and daikon (đồ chua) are used to add texture and additional flavor to a number of Vietnamese dishes, from sandwiches to vermicelli bowls. Its crunch and sweet-and-sour taste can make any savory dish more interesting, and its freshness can balance out the greasiness of fried food. To get that special crunch, all you need to do is let the carrots and daikon radishes sit in salt for a bit to draw out all the moisture.

SKILL LEVEL Basic | **YIELD** 1 (16-ounce/480-ml) glass jar

2 medium carrots, peeled and shredded or cut into sticks

2 medium daikon radishes, shredded or cut into sticks

2 teaspoons salt

2 tablespoons sugar

2 tablespoons white distilled or rice vinegar

1. In a medium bowl, toss carrots and daikon with the salt, and then let sit for 15 minutes. Rinse well and squeeze out all excess water.

2. Return the carrots and daikon to the bowl, add the sugar and vinegar, and toss well. Let sit for at least 30 minutes.

3. Store in a 16-ounce (480 ml) sterlized glass jar (page 34) or airtight container for up to 2 weeks in the refrigerator.

 NOTE *Daikon radishes have a sweet, yet spicy flavor. They are used in many Asian dishes and can also be served cooked or raw. You can find them at your local Asian grocery store, but they also might pop up occasionally at an organic or specialty market.*

PICKLED CABBAGE

This Vietnamese version of sauerkraut goes perfectly with braised or fried dishes. When served as a side dish for a weeknight family meal, bắp cải muối is often accompanied by a bowl of vegan fish dipping sauce. Rich in probiotics, vitamins, minerals, and fiber, this pickle helps maintain healthy gut flora and supports the immune system.

SKILL LEVEL Moderate | **YIELD** 2 (47-ounce/1.4-L) glass jars

BRINE

6 cups (1.5 L) water

1½ tablespoons salt

1 tablespoon sugar

½ cup (120 ml) rice rinse water

VEGETABLES

7 ounces (200 g) carrots, peeled and julienned (see Note on page 37)

1 small head white cabbage (about 1¾ pounds/800 g), thinly sliced

3 ounces (90 g) roughly chopped Vietnamese mint leaves

1. MAKE THE BRINE In a large saucepan, combine all ingredients except the rice water, and bring to a boil over high heat. Once salt and sugar are dissolved, remove from heat and let cool.

2. Stir in the rice water and then pour into jars with the vegetables you want to pickle.

3. PREP AND PACK THE VEGETABLES In a large bowl, combine all ingredients and mix well.

4. Place carrots, cabbage, and mint leaves in two 47-ounce (1.4 L) sterilized glass jars (see below) and cover with brine. Use two bamboo skewers to press the vegetables into the brine until completely submerged.

5. Close the lid tightly and leave jar undisturbed in a cool place for 2 to 3 days.

6. When pickled and sour enough to your liking, store in the refrigerator for up to 1 month.

HOW TO PROPERLY STERILIZE JARS

To ensure successful fermentation, make sure all your utensils and pans are clean and grease-free. You'll also want to thoroughly clean and sterilize your pickling jars, whether you've bought new ones or you have some you want to reuse. Luckily, you don't need any special tools, chemicals, or equipment to do so—just follow these simple steps:

- Wash jars and lids in hot, soapy water, and then rinse thoroughly.

- Place empty jars, open end up, in a large pot. Fill with hot water until covered, and then bring to a boil over high heat.

- Cover and continue to boil for 10 to 15 minutes.

- Using jar lifters or tongs, remove each jar, drain, and set on a cooling rack or heat-safe surface to dry.

PICKLED MUNG BEAN SPROUTS

Fresh mung bean sprouts are fragile and bulky, so you'll get better results
if you let them wilt in brine for a couple of hours before canning. You can serve
pickled mung bean sprouts (dưa giá) with braised or grilled dishes, or
accompanied by a bowl of vegan fish dipping sauce.

SKILL LEVEL Moderate | **YIELD** 2 (32-ounce/1-L) glass jars

BRINE

1 cup (240 ml) water

1 cup (240 ml) distilled
white vinegar

½ cup (100 g) sugar

½ teaspoon salt

VEGETABLES

3½ ounces (100 g) garlic chives
(or Chinese chives), cut into
3-inch (7.5 cm) lengths

1 cup (150 g) peeled and
julienned carrots (see Note)

2 red serrano or cayenne
peppers, julienned (see Note)

1 thumb-size piece ginger,
julienned (see Note)

17½ ounces (500 g) mung
bean sprouts

1. MAKE THE BRINE Combine all ingredients for the brine in a medium bowl
and stir until solids are dissolved.

2. PREP AND PACK THE VEGETABLES In a large bowl, mix garlic chives,
carrots, peppers, ginger, and mung bean sprouts, and then cover with brine.
Allow them to sit until the sprouts wilt (1 to 2 hours), after which, they will be
ready to eat.

3. Pack vegetables into a clean 32-ounce (1 L) sterilized glass jar (page 34) or
airtight container. Pour in just enough brine to cover, and then push them down
with two bamboo skewers to ensure the vegetables are fully submerged. Close
the lid tightly and store in the refrigerator for up to 2 weeks. (If the mung bean
sprouts start to turn too sour while you're storing them, simply drain the brine.)

🍂 **NOTE** *To julienne your vegetables, cut them into ⅛-inch (3 mm) thick slices,
then stack the slices and cut them into thin, matchstick-size pieces. To prep
the peppers, cut off the tops and bottoms, and use the tip of a knife to slice
down the sides and open them. Remove and discard the cores, place them
flat on a cutting board, then cut them into thin matchstick-size pieces.*

SALADS, WRAPS & ROLLS

If you have never tasted seaweed with jackfruit, tofu with betel leaf, or indulged in the visual wonder of a five-color salad, this section is for you! I have also included tasty vegan substitutes for fish and chicken salads. But of course, no Vietnamese cookbook would be complete without some delicious spring rolls; whether you prefer them crispy, green, or made with corn, you will find them all here.

VEGAN CHICKEN SALAD

For this recipe (gỏi gà chay), you'll use seitan as a chicken substitute because, when pan-fried, it develops a golden-brown, crispy crust that resembles chicken skin. Its inner texture is also white, soft, and slightly chewy, just like chicken meat.

SKILL LEVEL Moderate | **YIELD** 2 servings

SALAD

5 tablespoons vegetable oil, divided

10½ ounces (300 g) store-bought or homemade seitan (page 12)

1 leek (white part only), thinly sliced

½ teaspoon freshly ground black pepper

1¾ ounces (50 g) Vietnamese mint, stems removed and roughly chopped

3 makrut lime leaves, cut into fine threads

DRESSING

1 tablespoon sugar

1 tablespoon lime juice

1 teaspoon soy sauce

½ teaspoon salt

½ teaspoon vegetable or mushroom stock powder (optional)

1. MAKE THE SALAD In a medium skillet, heat 2 tablespoons of vegetable oil over low heat. When hot, add seitan and cook until golden brown on all sides (3 to 5 minutes). Remove and place on a paper towel–lined plate to drain and let cool.

2. Tear seitan into thin strips along fiber grain, place in a medium bowl, and set aside.

3. In a medium skillet, heat remaining 3 tablespoons of vegetable oil over medium heat. When hot, add leek and cook and stir until golden brown (1 to 2 minutes). Remove from heat and let cool.

4. MAKE THE DRESSING In a small bowl, combine sugar, lime juice, soy sauce, salt, and stock powder (if using). Stir well until all solids are dissolved.

5. ASSEMBLE Pour half of the dressing into the bowl of shredded seitan and mix well so seitan will absorb it.

6. Add fried leek, pepper, Vietnamese mint, lime leaves, and the rest of the dressing. Mix well and serve immediately.

LOTUS STEM AND SEAWEED SALAD

Lotus stems, or rootlets, come from lotus flowers. Their crunchy, yet tender, texture is perfect for salads and stir-fried dishes. You can find them pickled in brine in glass jars in the canned food section of most Asian grocery stores. I also use fried lotus roots (the chubby, underground stems, or rhizomes) in this salad to diversify the texture and add some interesting visuals to the presentation.

SKILL LEVEL Basic | **YIELD** 3 or 4 servings

10½ ounces (300 g) pickled lotus stems

1 small carrot, peeled and shredded

2 tablespoons sugar

Pinch of salt

2 teaspoons vegetable or mushroom stock powder, plus more to taste

3½ ounces (100 g) lotus root, peeled

3 tablespoons all-purpose flour

½ cup (120 ml) vegetable oil

¼ ounce (7 g) dried, seasoned laver seaweed (see Note)

1 ounce (28 g) mint leaves, roughly chopped

1 ounce (28 g) Vietnamese mint, roughly chopped

1. Rinse lotus stems well, drain, and place in a large bowl. Add the carrot, sugar, salt, and stock powder, and then toss well. Set aside for 10 minutes to allow the lotus stems to absorb all the seasonings.

2. With a sharp knife or mandoline, cut the lotus roots crosswise into ⅛-inch (3 mm) thick slices.

3. Put flour on a plate, coat lotus root slices in it, and shake off excess.

4. In a medium skillet, heat oil over medium heat. When hot, carefully drop in lotus root slices and fry until golden brown on both sides (about 2 minutes per side).

5. Using a slotted spoon, transfer lotus root slices to a paper towel–lined plate to drain.

6. In a large bowl, combine lotus stems, fried lotus root slices, seaweed, mint, and Vietnamese mint. Toss well, taste, and add more stock powder as needed.

7. Transfer salad to bowls and serve.

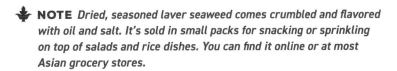 **NOTE** *Dried, seasoned laver seaweed comes crumbled and flavored with oil and salt. It's sold in small packs for snacking or sprinkling on top of salads and rice dishes. You can find it online or at most Asian grocery stores.*

YOUNG JACKFRUIT AND SEAWEED SALAD

Jackfruit is a large, heavy tropical fruit with a thick, bumpy rind. Because it's native to Asia, Africa, and South America, it's not readily available in other countries; however, for this recipe, you can use canned young jackfruit in brine, which you should be able to find at most Asian grocery stores. Just make sure you get green jackfruit, not yellow. You can also substitute an equal amount of breadfruit if you're unable to find green jackfruit. This recipe (gỏi rong biển mít non) also calls for fried leek, which make this dish far more flavorful.

SKILL LEVEL Moderate | **YIELD** 3 or 4 servings

10½ ounces (300 g) fresh young green jackfruit or breadfruit, peeled, or canned jackfruit, drained

½ teaspoon salt

3 tablespoons vegetable oil

3 ounces (90 g) thinly sliced leek (white part only)

1 teaspoon vegetable or mushroom stock powder

2 tablespoons roasted peanuts, crushed

1 tablespoon toasted sesame seeds, plus 1 teaspoon for garnish (optional)

1 ounce (28 g) mint

1 ounce (28 g) dried, seasoned seaweed crumbs (see Note), plus more to taste

1 bird's eye chili pepper, thinly sliced, for garnish (optional)

Sesame rice crackers, for serving (optional)

1. Place the young jackfruit in a pot, add salt, and then boil until soft enough to be easily skewered with a fork or chopstick (20 to 25 minutes for fresh or 15 minutes for canned; if using breadfruit, boil for 10 to 15 minutes). Remove from heat and allow to cool.

2. Cut jackfruit into thin slices, stack them on top of each other, and then cut along the grain into julienned strips (see Note on page 37).

3. Set a fine-mesh sieve over a heatproof bowl near the stovetop. Heat vegetable oil in a small skillet over medium heat. When hot, add leek and cook and stir until golden brown (about 2 minutes). Immediately empty contents of skillet into the fine-mesh sieve and set aside.

4. In a large bowl, combine jackfruit, stock powder, and 1 tablespoon of the fried leek oil. Mix thoroughly until jackfruit absorbs all seasonings.

5. Add peanuts, sesame seeds, mint, and seasoned seaweed, and mix well. Add more seasoned seaweed to taste.

6. Transfer salad to plates. Garnish with more sesame seeds and chili slices (if using) and serve with sesame rice crackers (if using).

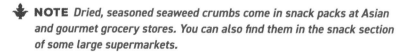 **NOTE** *Dried, seasoned seaweed crumbs come in snack packs at Asian and gourmet grocery stores. You can also find them in the snack section of some large supermarkets.*

VEGAN DRIED FISH AND BITTER MELON SALAD

In gỏi khổ qua cá chay, dried bean curd replaces the dried fish. You can use karela (Indian bitter melon) or Chinese bitter melon for this recipe. Karela has a darker-green skin and tighter, more pronounced bumps while the Chinese melon is lighter green and has wider, shallower bumps. To help reduce the bitterness of the melon, see step 4 below.

SKILL LEVEL Moderate | **YIELD** 4 servings

VEGAN DRIED FISH

4 cubes store-bought or homemade chao (page 22)

1 tablespoon sugar

1 teaspoon vegetable or mushroom stock powder

2 tablespoons all-purpose flour

3½ ounces (100 g) dried bean curd sticks, soaked (page 10)

1 cup (240 ml) vegetable oil

SALAD

1 large or 2 small karela or Chinese bitter melons, seeds removed and thinly sliced

1 small carrot, peeled and shredded

½ tablespoon salt

1¾ ounces (50 g) round leaf mint or mint, roughly chopped if leaves are large

1¾ ounces (50 g) cilantro, roughly chopped

3½ ounces (100 g) pickled scallion heads (optional; see Note)

3 tablespoons crushed roasted peanuts

Sesame rice crackers, for serving (optional)

SALAD DRESSING

1 tablespoon soy sauce

1 tablespoon sugar

2 teaspoons lime juice

1. MAKE THE VEGAN DRIED FISH In a medium bowl, mash the chao cubes with a spoon until it's a smooth paste. Add sugar and stock powder, and mix well. Add flour and stir briskly until you get a thick, smooth, homogenous mixture.

2. Spread a thin layer of the mixture on each dried bean curd stick.

3. Fill the bottom of a saucepan with about 2 inches (5 cm) of oil and place over medium heat. Check with a cooking thermometer and when oil reaches 320°F (160°C), add dried bean curd sticks and deep-fry until crisp and golden brown (1 to 2 minutes). Remove fried bean curd sticks, drain excess oil, and then cut into small pieces (about 2-inches/5-cm long).

4. MAKE THE SALAD Scrape all seeds and white spongy part off melons, slice them thinly crosswise, and then rinse a few times. (Optional: To reduce the bitterness, you can blanch the slices, and then drain.)

5. Toss bitter melons, carrots, and salt in a large bowl, and let sit for 15 minutes.

6. Rinse, squeeze out excess water, and then place in a large bowl.

7. MAKE THE DRESSING In a small bowl, combine soy sauce, sugar, and lime juice, and stir well until sugar is dissolved.

8. Add the dressing to the bowl with the salad mixture and toss well.

9. Add mint, cilantro, dried fish, pickled scallion heads (if using), and roasted peanuts, and mix together.

10. Serve with sesame rice crackers (if using).

NOTE *Pickled scallion heads (củ kiệu chua) make a nice addition to this recipe if you can find them at your local Asian grocery store.*

FIVE-COLOR SALAD

The core of Vietnamese cuisine is made up of the power of five flavors, which correspond to the five elements: spicy (metal), sour (wood), bitter (fire), salty (water), and sweet (earth). Likewise, many chefs strive to feature five colors in their dishes that correspond to the gastronomic senses: sight, touch, smell, sound, and taste. This salad (gỏi ngũ sắc) is the perfect example of this meticulous philosophy. It's so colorful and will look fantastic on your party or banquet table, but it's also simple enough to prepare for a weeknight meal.

SKILL LEVEL Basic | **YIELD** 4 servings

4 tablespoons vegetable oil, divided

1 block (14 ounces/400 g) firm tofu

3½ ounces (100 g) leek (white part only), thinly sliced

1 cube store-bought or homemade chao (page 22)

1 tablespoon fermented soybean sauce

1 tablespoon sriracha

2 teaspoons sugar

1 tablespoon lime juice

1 tablespoon sesame or olive oil

1 bird's eye chili pepper, minced, plus more sliced for garnish

3 ounces (90 g) banana blossom, prepped (page 15) and thinly sliced (optional)

3 ounces (90 g) cucumber, seeds removed and thinly sliced

3 ounces (90 g) carrot, peeled and shredded

3 ounces (90 g) red cabbage, shredded

1 ounce (28 g) mint

3 tablespoons roasted peanuts, crushed

2 tablespoons toasted sesame seeds

1. In a medium skillet, heat 1 tablespoon of vegetable oil over medium heat. When hot, add tofu and cook until golden brown on all sides (about 10 minutes). Place tofu on paper towel–lined plate to drain.

2. Cut tofu into thin strips and set aside.

3. In a clean skillet, heat remaining 3 tablespoons of vegetable oil, and then cook and stir sliced leek until golden brown (about 2 minutes). Using a slotted spoon, transfer leek to a paper towel–lined plate to drain.

4. In a small bowl, mash the chao into a smooth paste, and then add fermented soybean and sriracha sauces, sugar, lime juice, sesame oil, and minced chili pepper, and stir well.

5. Arrange banana blossom slices (if using), cucumber, carrot, cabbage, and mint on a platter. Top with tofu, and then sprinkle with fried leek, peanuts, and sesame seeds.

6. Drizzle dressing on top, garnish with chili slices, and toss well before serving.

CRISPY SPRING ROLLS

I'm often asked why spring rolls in other countries aren't as golden, flaky, and crispy as those in Vietnam. The secret lies in the variety of spring roll wrappers we use here. The most common—bánh đa nem in the North and bánh tráng lề in the Central areas—are as thin as carbon paper. The only problem is that these wrappers are difficult to store and keep fresh, so few Asian grocery stores outside of Vietnam carry them. However, you can substitute Chinese spring roll pastry wrappers or Vietnamese rice paper wrappers to make these rolls. Also, be sure to check out the Tips for Crispier Spring Rolls on page 52. This recipe was inspired by chả giò, deep-fried spring rolls from South Vietnam.

SKILL LEVEL Advanced | **YIELD** 20 spring rolls

½ recipe mashed mung beans (page 11)

2 tablespoons vegetable oil, plus more for deep-frying

2 tablespoons minced leek (white part only) or scallion

½ cup (44 g) finely chopped straw or brown mushrooms

¼ cup (22 g) dried shiitake mushrooms, soaked (page 12) and chopped

½ cup (44 g) dried wood ear mushrooms, soaked (page 13) and finely chopped

1 cup (250 g) glass noodles, soaked until soft, drained, and roughly chopped

1 cup (100 g) finely shredded taro (page 17)

1 cup (100 g) peeled and shredded carrot

½ teaspoon salt

1 teaspoon sugar, plus 1 tablespoon for soaking rice paper

1 teaspoon vegetable or mushroom stock powder

continued on following page

1. Put mashed mung beans in a large bowl and set aside.

2. Heat 2 tablespoons of vegetable oil in a small skillet over low heat. When hot, add leek and cook and stir until slightly golden brown (about 1 minute). Remove from heat and transfer both vegetables and oil to bowl of mashed mung beans.

3. Add mushrooms, glass noodles, taro, carrot, salt, 1 teaspoon of sugar, stock powder, and pepper. Mix well and set aside.

4. Prepare rice paper wrappers for rolling with the lime juice, water, and 1 tablespoon of sugar (page 11). Place a wrapper on a flat surface and add 1 tablespoon of filling closer to one end. Lift up that end, fold it, push the filling back a little bit, and then fold in both sides. Continue to roll tightly all the way to the other end. Repeat with remaining wrappers and filling.

5. Line a medium saucepan with parchment paper to prevent rolls from picking up any burnt bits from the bottom. Fill with 2 inches (5 cm) of oil. Heat oil to 350°F (175°C). (You can check the temperature with a cooking thermometer or insert one end of a chopstick in the oil; if bubbles appear around it, the oil is ready for deep-frying).

6. Fry rolls in batches of 5 to 8 over medium-low heat until golden brown (about 10 minutes). The rice paper might be sticky at first, so be sure to leave some space between each roll.

continued from previous page

½ teaspoon freshly ground
black pepper

20 rice paper or spring roll
wrappers (6 inches/15 cm)

1 tablespoon lime juice,
for soaking rice paper

2 cups (480 ml) water,
to soften rice paper

Vegan fish dipping sauce
(page 20), for serving

7. Using a wire spider or slotted spoon, transfer rolls to a cooling rack or paper towel–lined plate to drain.

8. Serve within 1 hour of frying with vegan fish dipping sauce.

TIPS FOR CRISPIER SPRING ROLLS

A good spring roll should be evenly golden and crispy, and remain that way even after a few hours. The filling should be succulent, but not soggy. The following tips will help you achieve the best results when making crispy spring rolls.

WRAPPING

It shows off your technique when you can produce a crispy spring roll that is neither too sticky nor too sloppy. Wheat-flour wrappers are an easy option, as they deep-fry crispy and golden with no extra effort. Another popular and efficient type of wrapper is made from wheat and mung bean (bánh tráng pía đậu xanh). But if you want to make authentic Vietnamese spring rolls, follow these tips to successfully wrap them with rice paper:

- Do not soak rice paper in water, as it becomes too soft and wet to work with; instead, slightly wet the cutting board and place the rice paper on top. By the time you finish spooning on the filling, it should be soft enough to roll. Alternatively, place the rice paper inside a folded, damp cloth for a couple of seconds.

- For nice and even golden-brown rolls, use Coca-Cola, Sarsi (a Southeast Asian sarsaparilla soft drink), beer, or coconut water to wet the rice paper. The sugar content in these liquids caramelizes under high oil temperatures, browning the rolls nicely.

- When you're done wrapping, roll each spring roll back and forth under your palm on the counter to release the air bubbles inside. This prevents bubbles from forming on the skin of the rolls.

- Place the rolls in the refrigerator for 2 hours before frying, so the rice paper has time to dry.

FILLING

- Some filling ingredients, such as bean sprouts, jicama, and carrots, might release their juices during frying, which leaves the rolls not as crispy as you want. To prevent this, mix these ingredients with some sugar and squeeze out the excess moisture after letting them sit for 15 minutes.

FRYING

When it's time to fry your spring rolls, these tips will ensure a crispy result every time:

- Make sure there is enough frying oil to fully cover the rolls.

- Add a few drops of fresh lime juice to the frying oil to make the rolls crispier.

- Fry over medium-low heat—the temperature of the oil should be 350°F (175°C).

- Double frying is always the secret to keeping fried food crispy for a long time. First, fry on medium-low to cook the fillings, and then fry again on medium-high to brown the crust.

- You can freeze the rolls after the first fry, but do not defrost for the second; just drop them into the oil frozen.

- After frying, drain off excess oil by standing the rolls up on a frying rack or placing them on paper towels. Do not turn off the heat and leave the rolls in the oil as they will turn soggy.

GREEN FRESH SPRING ROLLS

Green fresh spring rolls (cuốn diếp) are light and incredibly refreshing on hot days. I first tried this dish at a vegan restaurant in Ho Chi Minh City and was amazed at how tasty it was. Mustard greens (*Brassica jucea*) refer to a variety of plants that differ sharply in heat, flavor, and appearance. This recipe calls for cải cay (Vietnamese) or juk gai choy (Cantonese), which is a leafy, light green romaine with a narrow, celery-shaped stem. It supplies a remarkable peppery taste with just a hint of mustard.

SKILL LEVEL Moderate | **YIELD** 4 servings

SPRING ROLLS

7 ounces (200 g) firm tofu

¼ cup (60 ml) plus 1 tablespoon vegetable oil, divided

1 tablespoon minced scallion (white part only), plus 5 scallions (green parts only)

3½ ounces (100 g) peeled and shredded carrot, divided

1½ ounces (45 g) dried wood ear, oyster, or shiitake mushrooms (page 12), cut into ¼-inch (6 mm) strips

1½ teaspoons sugar, divided

1 teaspoon vegetable or mushroom stock powder

¼ teaspoon salt

1 tablespoon distilled white vinegar

7 ounces (200 g) dried rice vermicelli noodles

2 sweet potatoes, boiled until tender and cut into sticks about the size of french fries

3½ ounces (100 g) fresh herbs (such as mint, Asian basil, and/or perilla leaves)

1 pound (454 g) fresh mustard greens (cải cay or juk gai choy; see Note on page 54), thick part of stems removed and rinsed

continued on following page

1. MAKE THE SPRING ROLLS Cut the tofu into ½-inch (1 cm) thick "steaks."

2. In a medium skillet, heat ¼ cup (60 ml) of the vegetable oil over medium heat. When hot, cook the tofu in batches until golden brown on both sides (5 to 8 minutes per side). When done, transfer tofu to a paper towel–lined plate to drain. Let cool completely, and then cut the steaks into ½-inch (1 cm) wide sticks.

3. Discard remaining oil in skillet, add remaining 1 tablespoon vegetable oil and heat over low heat. Add 1 tablespoon of minced scallion (white part) and cook and stir until golden brown (about 1 minute).

4. Add half the carrot and cook and stir until softened (1 to 2 minutes). Add mushrooms, ½ teaspoon of the sugar, stock powder, and salt, and stir well. Add the prepared tofu, gently toss to combine, and then transfer to a plate to cool.

5. In a medium bowl, combine remaining carrot with remaining 1 teaspoon sugar and vinegar. Mix well and set aside for 10 minutes.

6. Fill a medium saucepan halfway with water and bring to a rolling boil over high heat. Prepare a bowl of ice water and set nearby. Drop scallions (green part) into boiling water for 30 seconds, or until wilted. Use a wire spider or slotted spoon to transfer to bowl of ice water. Drain and set aside.

7. Cook the dried vermicelli noodles following package instructions.

8. Place tofu-mushroom mixture, sweet potatoes, fresh herbs, noodles, mustard greens, and green scallions on separate plates.

continued from previous page

DIPPING SAUCE

1 tablespoon vegetable oil

1 tablespoon minced scallion
(white part only)

¼ cup (120 ml) fermented
soybean sauce

¼ cup (50 g) sugar

1 tablespoon peanut butter

½ cup (120 ml) water

¼ cup (32 g) toasted
sesame seeds

1 bird's eye chili pepper,
minced (optional)

9. Place one mustard green leaf, dark side down, on a flat work surface or cutting board. Place a bit of each filling ingredient—rice vermicelli, 1 tablespoon of tofu-mushroom mixture, 1 sweet potato stick, pickled carrot, and fresh herbs—on one end of the leaf. Lift up the end with the fillings over the fillings, and then gently roll it up.

10. Use a leaf layer of blanched scallion as a string to tie up the roll, and then repeat with the remaining mustard leaves, fillings, and scallions. Lay the rolls parallel to each other and trim off the top and bottom edges to make them uniform in size.

11. MAKE THE DIPPING SAUCE In a small saucepan, heat 1 tablespoon of vegetable oil over low heat. When hot, add 1 tablespoon of minced scallion and cook and stir until fragrant (about 30 seconds).

12. Add fermented soybean sauce, ¼ cup (50 g) of sugar, peanut butter, and water, and stir well. Simmer until smooth and thickened (1 to 2 minutes).

13. Transfer to a dipping sauce bowl, stir in sesame seeds, top with minced chili pepper (if using) and serve with green spring rolls.

NOTE *You can find mustard greens in the fresh produce section of most Asian grocery stores. As a substitute, you can use greens such as Batavia lettuce, green leaf lettuce, kale, or Swiss chard.*

CORN SPRING ROLLS

Corn spring rolls (ram bắp) are a specialty of Quang Ngai, a town in Central Vietnam. They're crispy on the outside but slimmer and longer than Crispy Spring Rolls (page 51).

SKILL LEVEL Advanced | **YIELD** 20 spring rolls

2 glutinous or sweet corncobs (see Note)

1 ounce (28 g) dried wood ear mushrooms, soaked (page 13) and finely chopped

1 tablespoon chopped cilantro

7 ounces tofu (200 g), finely crumbled with a fork

1 ounce (28 g) leek (white part only), finely chopped

1 teaspoon sugar, plus 1 tablespoon for soaking rice paper wrappers

½ teaspoon salt

1 teaspoon vegetable or mushroom stock powder

Pinch of freshly ground black pepper

20 rice paper or spring roll wrappers (6 inches/15 cm)

1 tablespoon lime juice, for soaking rice paper

2 cups (480 ml) water, to soften rice paper

Vegetable oil, for deep-frying

½ cup (120 ml) vegan fish dipping sauce (page 20), for serving

1. Using a knife or mandoline, shave corn kernels off cobs into a bowl and set aside.

2. In a large bowl, combine mushrooms, cilantro, tofu, leek, 1 teaspoon of sugar, salt, stock powder, and pepper. Mix well and set aside for 15 minutes.

3. Prepare rice paper wrappers for rolling with the lime juice, water, and 1 tablespoon of sugar (page 11).

4. To assemble the rolls, scoop 1 tablespoon of filling on one end of a wrapper, and then spread until it covers about 4 inches (10 cm), leaving some room on the sides. Lift that end of the wrapper and fold it over the filling. Push the covered filling back a bit, and then fold in both sides. Continue to roll tightly to the other end. Repeat with the remaining wrappers and filling.

5. Cut a piece of parchment paper to line the bottom of a medium saucepan or skillet. Fill the bottom of the saucepan with 2 inches (5 cm) of oil and heat to 360°F (180°C). (You can check the temperature with a cooking thermometer or insert one end of a chopstick in the oil; if bubbles appear around it, the oil is ready for deep-frying.)

6. Drop rolls in the pan, seam sides down so that they remain sealed when they touch the hot oil. Deep-fry in batches until golden brown (5 to 8 minutes). When done, use a wire spider or slotted spoon to transfer rolls to a cooling rack or paper towel–lined plate to drain.

7. Serve warm with vegan fish dipping sauce.

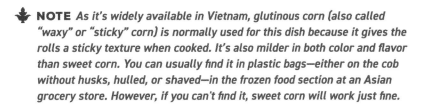 **NOTE** *As it's widely available in Vietnam, glutinous corn (also called "waxy" or "sticky" corn) is normally used for this dish because it gives the rolls a sticky texture when cooked. It's also milder in both color and flavor than sweet corn. You can usually find it in plastic bags—either on the cob without husks, hulled, or shaved—in the frozen food section at an Asian grocery store. However, if you can't find it, sweet corn will work just fine.*

TOFU WRAPPED IN WILD BETEL LEAF

This is a vegan version of beef wrapped in wild betel leaf (bò lá lốt), a popular and delicious street snack from Southern Vietnam. Wild betel leaves, or lá lốt, are not the same as piper betel, or lá trầu, which is commonly chewed to freshen the breath. These rolls can be served as an appetizer with some fresh greens and any vegan dipping sauce. You can also serve them with rice or on top of a bowl of vermicelli noodles with fresh greens, grilled seitan and mushrooms, some Pickled Carrots and Daikon (page 33), and a side of Vegan Fish Dipping Sauce (page 20).

SKILL LEVEL Moderate | **YIELD** 25 to 30 rolls

21 ounces (595 g) firm tofu

30 to 35 wild betel leaves (see Note), divided

1 ounce (28 g) dried shiitake mushrooms, soaked (page 12) and minced

½ ounce (14 g) dried wood ear mushrooms, soaked (page 13) and minced

1 tablespoon minced lemongrass

½ teaspoon five-spice powder

½ teaspoon salt

½ teaspoon vegetable or mushroom stock powder

1 teaspoon sugar

2 tablespoons vegetable oil, for brushing, plus more if needed

1 tablespoon crushed roasted peanuts, for garnish

½ cup (120 ml) vegan fish dipping sauce (page 20), for serving

1. In a large bowl, mash tofu blocks with a fork into fine crumbles.

2. Cut 5 wild betel leaves into fine strips and add to the tofu, along with mushrooms, lemongrass, five-spice powder, salt, stock powder, and sugar. Mix well and set aside for 15 minutes.

3. Place a wild betel leaf, shiny side down, on your work surface with the tip of the leaf at the top. Place 1 tablespoon of filling near the tip. Starting from the tip, roll tightly into a cigar shape. When you reach the stem end, use a toothpick to punch a hole in the middle of the roll. Insert the leaf stem into the hole to secure. Repeat with remaining leaves and filling.

4. Brush the rolls all over with vegetable oil. Place them on grilling skewers, 5 rolls per skewer, working with one roll at a time, with the skewer going through the stem in the center.

5. Grill on an outdoor charcoal grill until leaves start to wrinkle (about 10 minutes), flipping and brushing with more oil about halfway through. Alternatively, bake them in the oven at 350°F (175°C) until the leaves start to wrinkle (15 to 20 minutes, flipping and brushing with more oil about halfway through). You can also fry the rolls in 3 tablespoons of vegetable oil in a large skillet over medium heat until the leaves start to wrinkle (2 to 3 minutes per side).

6. Arrange on a platter, garnish with crushed roasted peanuts, and serve with vegan fish dipping sauce.

 NOTE *You can buy fresh wild betel leaves at most Asian grocery stores. They're heart-shaped and a glossy dark green on one side, and a matte, lighter green on the other. They provide a pleasant peppery flavor. To make them pliable and easier to roll, heat in the microwave on high for 10 seconds or hold them briefly over an open flame with a pair of tongs.*

BRAISED, FRIED, STIR-FRIED & GRILLED DISHES

We could all use some more go-to weeknight recipes, and you're sure to find some delicious options in this section. With savory substitutions, like tofu, seitan, and mushrooms, bathed in delicious sweet-and-sour or spicy sauces, no one will even notice they are eating a vegan dish. You don't have to keep it in the kitchen either—fire up that grill and serve up some incredible grilled eggplant at your next cookout.

SPICY TOFU

This dish (đậu phụ sốt cay) was inspired by the popular Chinese mapo tofu. Be sure to use silken tofu for better results. It can also be served as a side along with steamed rice.

SKILL LEVEL Moderate | **YIELD** 4 servings

2 tablespoons vegetable oil

1 teaspoon minced garlic

1 teaspoon minced shallot

1 teaspoon minced bird's eye chili pepper, plus sliced chili pepper for garnish (optional)

½ ounce (14 g) dried shiitake mushrooms, soaked (page 12) and minced

1 tablespoon chili jam (page 25) or hot sauce (such as sriracha or Korean hot pepper paste)

1 tablespoon soy sauce

1 tablespoon vegetarian oyster sauce

¼ cup (60 ml) water

1 tablespoon julienned ginger (see Note on page 37)

10½ ounces (300 g) silken tofu, cut into small cubes

1 tablespoon sugar

½ teaspoon vegetable or mushroom stock powder

½ teaspoon salt

½ teaspoon freshly ground black pepper

1 ounce (28 g) chopped cilantro, for garnish

1. In a large skillet or wok, heat oil over medium heat. Add garlic, shallot, and minced chili pepper, and cook and stir until garlic turns slightly golden on edges (about 30 seconds).

2. Add mushrooms, chili jam, soy sauce, and vegetarian oyster sauce, and mix well.

3. Stir in water and ginger.

4. Add tofu cubes, sugar, stock powder, and salt, and simmer until sauce slightly thickens (2 to 3 minutes).

5. Transfer to a platter, dust with ground pepper, garnish with chopped cilantro and sliced chili pepper (if using), and serve.

BRAISED YOUNG JACKFRUIT WITH LEMONGRASS AND CHILI

A typical Vietnamese family meal consists of steamed rice, a main dish (normally a fried or braised protein), a vegetable dish (boiled or stir-fried), a broth soup, some fresh vegetables and herbs or pickles, and dipping sauce. This recipe (mít non kho sả ớt) can be served as a main dish with a side of steamed rice. The lemongrass and chili peppers add aroma and flavor to the braised young jackfruit. Once you try it, it's sure to become a family favorite.

SKILL LEVEL Moderate	YIELD 4 servings

14 ounces (400 g) fresh young jackfruit or breadfruit, peeled, or canned jackfruit, drained

½ teaspoon salt

3 tablespoons vegetable oil

1 tablespoon minced lemongrass

3 bird's eye chili peppers, seeds removed and minced

1 tablespoon minced leek (white part only)

1 tablespoon sugar

2 tablespoons soy sauce

1 teaspoon vegetable or mushroom stock powder

½ teaspoon freshly ground black pepper

1 tablespoon chili jam (page 25) (optional)

½ cup (120 ml) water

1. If using breadfruit, skip to step 2. Place jackfruit in a medium saucepan and fill with enough water to cover. Add salt, bring to a boil over high heat, and then reduce to medium. Continue to cook until soft and easily skewered with a fork or chopstick (20 to 25 minutes for fresh or 15 minutes for canned). Transfer to a plate to cool.

2. Pat dry and cut jackfruit or breadfruit into ½-inch (1 cm) thick slices.

3. In a medium saucepan, heat vegetable oil over medium heat. Add lemongrass and minced chili peppers and leek, and cook and stir for 1 to 2 minutes.

4. When leek and lemongrass begin to turn golden brown, add jackfruit or breadfruit slices, and cook until golden brown on all sides (5 to 10 minutes). Remove from heat.

5. Add sugar, soy sauce, stock powder, pepper, and chili jam (if using). Toss well and let sit for 20 to 30 minutes to allow flavors to infuse.

6. Add ½ cup (120 ml) of water and simmer on low heat until sauce is reduced by one third (about 30 minutes).

7. Transfer to a platter and serve.

BRAISED BEANS IN COCONUT MILK WITH SHIITAKE MUSHROOMS

My mom makes this dish (đậu ngự rim dừa và nấm hương) quite often during the spring and summer, when fresh lima beans are in season. If you can't find fresh lima beans in your location, the dried kind will work as well. Just rehydrate them by soaking them in water overnight.

SKILL LEVEL Moderate | **YIELD** 4 servings

3½ ounces (100 g) fresh (or dried, soaked for 8 to 10 hours and drained) lima beans

3½ ounces (100 g) fresh (or dried, soaked for 8 to 10 hours and drained) pinto beans

Pinch of salt

2 tablespoons vegetable oil

1 tablespoon minced leek (white part only)

½ ounce (14 g) dried shiitake mushrooms, soaked (page 12) and large caps halved and small caps quartered

1 teaspoon soy sauce

3½ ounces (100 g) mature coconut meat (see Note), cut into thin, small slices

5½ ounces (165 ml) full-fat, unsweetened coconut milk

1 teaspoon vegetable or mushroom stock powder

1 ounce (28 g) ginger, julienned (see Note on page 37)

1 cube store-bought or homemade chao (page 22), mashed

½ teaspoon toasted black sesame seeds, for garnish

1. Fill a large saucepan halfway with water and bring to a boil over high heat. Add beans and salt, reduce the heat to medium, and cook until softened (about 15 minutes). Drain and transfer to a bowl.

2. In a medium skillet, heat vegetable oil over low heat. When hot, add leek and cook and stir until slightly golden around the edges (about 30 seconds). Add mushrooms and soy sauce and stir well. Add cooked beans, coconut meat and milk, and stock powder, and continue to cook, stirring often, until bubbly (about 3 minutes).

3. Stir in ginger and chao and continue to cook on low heat, stirring often, until slightly thickened (5 to 10 minutes). Remove from heat.

4. Transfer to serving bowls and sprinkle with black sesame seeds.

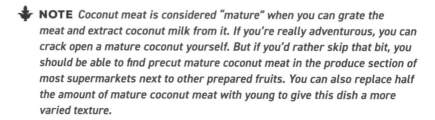 **NOTE** *Coconut meat is considered "mature" when you can grate the meat and extract coconut milk from it. If you're really adventurous, you can crack open a mature coconut yourself. But if you'd rather skip that bit, you should be able to find precut mature coconut meat in the produce section of most supermarkets next to other prepared fruits. You can also replace half the amount of mature coconut meat with young to give this dish a more varied texture.*

BRAISED TOFU WITH PINEAPPLE AND MUSHROOMS

Infused with shallots, black pepper, and soy sauce, this dish (đậu phụ kho thơm) is a celebration of textures. It also offers the perfect balance of sweet, sour, and hot! It makes an excellent side dish along with some steamed rice. To save some time, you can buy fried tofu at most Asian grocery stores.

SKILL LEVEL Basic | **YIELD** 4 servings

¼ cup (60 ml) plus 1 tablespoon vegetable oil, divided

1 block (14 ounces/400 g) firm tofu

½ teaspoon salt

½ teaspoon freshly ground black pepper, plus more for garnish

½ ounce (14 g) shallots, sliced

7 ounces (200 g) pineapple, cut into thin and quartered slices

1 teaspoon sugar

1 teaspoon vegetarian oyster sauce

1 teaspoon soy sauce

1 teaspoon sriracha sauce

2 tablespoons water

3½ ounces (100 g) straw or brown mushrooms, halved

1 small scallion, chopped, for garnish

1. Heat ¼ cup (60 ml) of the vegetable oil in a medium skillet over medium heat. Once hot, add tofu and cook until golden brown on all sides (10 to 15 minutes). Remove and place on a paper towel–lined plate to drain and let cool. Cut tofu into 1-inch (2.5 cm) cubes, and season with salt and pepper.

2. In a large skillet, heat remaining 1 tablespoon of vegetable oil over low heat. When hot, add shallots and cook and stir until slightly golden (about 30 seconds).

3. Add pineapple and sugar, and cook on medium-low heat until slightly caramelized (2 to 3 minutes).

4. Add the vegetarian oyster sauce, soy sauce, sriracha, water, tofu cubes, and mushrooms. Cover and braise for 10 minutes over low heat.

5. Transfer to a platter, dust with more ground pepper, garnish with chopped scallion, and serve.

SWEET-AND-SOUR SEITAN

The key to success with this dish (mì căn rim chua ngọt) is its flavorful sweet-and-sour sauce. If you're not a fan of seitan, feel free to use any other plant-based protein you prefer, such as vegan chicken tenders or chunks, or textured vegetable protein. Anything that has a chewy, springy texture to absorb the sauce will work.

SKILL LEVEL Basic | **YIELD** 4 servings

¼ cup (60 ml) vegetable oil

7 ounces (200 g) store-bought or homemade seitan (page 12) or vegan protein of choice

2 tablespoons white vinegar

2 tablespoons ketchup

1 tablespoon brown sugar

1 tablespoon vegetable or mushroom stock powder

1 teaspoon sesame oil

2 tablespoons soy sauce

1 tablespoon sriracha sauce

1 tablespoon vegetarian oyster sauce (optional)

½ cup (120 ml) water

½ teaspoon freshly ground black pepper, for garnish

1 tablespoon roasted sesame seeds, for garnish

1. In a medium skillet, heat oil over low heat. When hot, add seitan and cook until golden brown on all sides (3 to 5 minutes). Remove and place on a paper towel–lined plate to drain and let cool. Cut into ½-inch (1 cm) thick slices.

2. In a small bowl, whisk together vinegar, ketchup, brown sugar, stock powder, sesame oil, soy sauce, sriracha, and vegetarian oyster sauce (if using) until solids are dissolved.

3. Simmer seitan slices, prepared sauce, and water in a large skillet over medium-low heat until sauce thickens (about 15 minutes). Remove from heat.

4. Transfer to a platter, dust with pepper, sprinkle with sesame seeds, and serve.

BRAISED GINGER MUSHROOMS

King oyster mushrooms (also called king trumpet mushrooms), are the largest of the oyster mushroom genus. They have thick, white, nearly cylindrical (but smooth) stems and brown caps. They're a popular substitute for meat and seafood in vegan and vegetarian dishes due to their chewy texture and rich umami flavor. The "heating" (yang) properties of ginger in this recipe (nấm kho gừng) help balance out the "cooling" (yin) of the mushrooms.

SKILL LEVEL Moderate | **YIELD** 2 servings

7 ounces (200 g) king oyster mushrooms, rinsed and cut into bite-size pieces

1 teaspoon vegetable or mushroom stock powder

2 tablespoons soy sauce

1 tablespoon minced leek (white part only)

½ teaspoon freshly ground black pepper, plus more for garnish

2 tablespoons vegetable oil

1 tablespoon sugar

1 ounce (28 g) ginger, julienned (see Note on page 37), plus more for garnish

Sliced bird's eye chili pepper, for garnish (optional)

Cilantro, for garnish (optional)

1. In a large bowl, combine mushrooms, stock powder, soy sauce, leek, and pepper. Mix well and set aside for 15 minutes.

2. In a medium skillet, heat oil over low heat. When hot, add sugar and cook until melted and caramelized (1 to 2 minutes).

3. Add marinated mushrooms and ginger and stir well. Continue to cook over low heat until mushrooms are soft and sauce is reduced by half (about 10 minutes). Remove from heat.

4. Transfer to a platter; lightly dust with ground pepper; garnish with more ginger strips, sliced chili pepper (if using), and cilantro (if using); and serve.

JAPANESE-STYLE SAVORY AND SWEET TOFU

A Japanese friend shared this recipe (đậu phụ mặn ngọt kiểu Nhật) with me, and it has since become one of my favorite tofu dishes. The tofu is wrapped in roasted nori (dried seaweed) strips, pan-fried until crispy, and coated in a sweet and savory teriyaki glaze. When it's done, it's sticky-crisp on the outside and tender on the inside. The nori adds a "just right" hint of seafood flavor.

SKILL LEVEL Moderate | **YIELD** 4 servings

TOFU

1 block (14 ounces/400 g) firm tofu

1 sheet (7 by 8 inches/20 by 22 cm) roasted nori

3 tablespoons cornstarch

½ cup (120 ml) vegetable oil

1 teaspoon toasted sesame seeds, for garnish

SAUCE

2 tablespoons soy sauce

1 tablespoon sugar

2 tablespoons Chinese rice cooking wine or water

1 teaspoon grated ginger

1. MAKE THE TOFU Cut tofu into 2 by 3-inch (5 by 7.5 cm) pieces that are ½ inch (1 cm) thick. Cut nori sheets into strips that are 6 inches (15 cm) long and ¼ inch (6 mm) wide. Wrap a piece of tofu in each strip. The moisture on the tofu should help the seaweed to adhere to it, but if it doesn't, use your finger to dab a tiny bit of water on the edge of the seaweed strip until it seals securely.

2. Sprinkle cornstarch on a small rimmed plate, roll each piece of nori-tofu in it, and then gently shake off the excess.

3. Fill the bottom of a large skillet with vegetable oil about 1 inch (2.5 cm) deep and heat over medium-low heat. After about 3 minutes, check the oil with a food thermometer to see if it has reached 320°F (160°C). (You can also dip the pointy end of a wooden chopstick in the oil; if a steady stream of bubbles appears, it's ready.) Carefully drop in nori-tofu, cooking in batches if necessary, and fry until golden brown on both sides (about 8 minutes). With a slotted spoon, transfer tofu to a paper towel–lined plate to drain.

4. MAKE THE SAUCE In a medium pan, combine soy sauce, sugar, cooking wine, and ginger (see Note). Simmer over medium-low heat, stirring constantly, until slightly thickened (1 to 2 minutes).

5. Add the deep-fried tofu to the sauce and toss well.

6. Transfer to a platter, sprinkle with toasted sesame seeds, and serve.

🌿 **NOTE** *When you first combine the ingredients for the sauce, there will be a bit of smoke, but don't be alarmed—just keep stirring.*

GRILLED EGGPLANT

For this recipe (cà tím nướng mỡ hành), you will need a gas or charcoal grill. I use Japanese eggplants, which are an oblong shape and dark purple in color. They have a delicate, spongy texture and offer an incredible smoky flavor when grilled. Be sure to choose some that feel sturdy and dense and have a smooth exterior. Avoid any that have bruises or soft spots.

SKILL LEVEL Moderate | **YIELD** 4 servings

3 Japanese eggplants or 1 medium globe eggplant (see Note)

2 cloves garlic

1 bird's eye chili pepper, chopped

2 tablespoons plus 1 teaspoon sugar, divided

3 tablespoons vegan fish sauce (page 20)

3½ ounces (100 g) chopped scallions

3 tablespoons vegetable oil

1 tablespoon fried shallots (see step 1 on page 127 or store-bought), for garnish (optional)

1 tablespoon crushed roasted peanuts, for garnish (optional)

1. Using a skewer or toothpick, poke holes all over the surface of each eggplant.

2. If using a gas grill, preheat it to 500°F (250°C). Using tongs, place each eggplant on the hot grill and close the lid. Check after 10 minutes and again after 15 minutes. If eggplants look deflated and their grilled sides are soft (use a toothpick to check), they're ready to be flipped. Grill for another 10 minutes, or until all flesh has collapsed and turned soft. If using a charcoal grill, grease the grate, then heat to medium-high heat (that is, coals should be covered with ash and glowing red without any black remaining). Using tongs, place each eggplant on the hot grate and cook them uncovered, turning occasionally, until skin is blackened and flesh has collapsed (15 to 20 minutes). Remove from grill and allow to cool.

3. Carefully remove skin from eggplants, leaving the stems intact, and then arrange on a platter. Loosely drag a fork through the flesh to loosen so it will absorb the sauce.

4. In a food processor or mortar and pestle, combine the garlic, chili, and 1 teaspoon of the sugar, and grind into a coarse paste.

5. In a small bowl, mix remaining 2 tablespoons sugar and vegan fish sauce, and stir until sugar is dissolved. Add garlic-chili paste and mix well.

6. Place the scallions in a small, heatproof bowl. Heat oil in a small skillet over medium heat. When it starts to smoke, immediately remove from heat, pour the oil over the scallions, and stir well.

7. Drizzle sauce all over eggplants and top them off with some of the scallion oil.

8. Garnish with fried shallots (if using) and roasted peanuts (if using).

NOTE *If using a globe eggplant, the cooking time will likely be much longer (up to 1 hour, depending on the size). Because globe eggplants are larger than Japanese ones, slice in half lengthwise before serving.*

OYSTER MUSHROOM STIR-FRY WITH TURMERIC

This is the vegan version of stir-fried intestine with turmeric (lòng xào nghệ)—a popular specialty dish in Central Vietnam. The seitan in Vietnam comes in a tube shape, so it looks quite similar to the meat in the original dish when it's cut into rings, but you can omit this ingredient if you prefer.

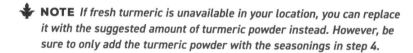

SKILL LEVEL Moderate | **YIELD** 2 servings

7 ounces (200 g) oyster mushrooms, rinsed with salted water

3-inch (7.5 cm) piece fresh turmeric, peeled, or 1 teaspoon turmeric powder (see Note)

2 tablespoons vegetable oil

2 cloves garlic, minced

3 ounces (90 g) store-bought or homemade seitan (page 12), cut into ¼-inch (6 mm) thick rings (optional)

½ teaspoon salt

½ teaspoon sugar

½ teaspoon vegetable or mushroom stock powder

½ teaspoon freshly ground black pepper

1 ounce (28 g) cilantro or Vietnamese mint leaves, for garnish

2 tablespoons crushed peanuts, for garnish

Sliced bird's eye chili pepper, for garnish (optional)

1. Tear mushrooms lengthwise into quarters, squeeze out excess water, and set aside.

2. Cut turmeric into smaller chunks, place in a resealable plastic bag, and crush finely with a pestle. Transfer to a bowl and set aside.

3. In a large skillet, heat vegetable oil over low heat. When hot, add garlic and cook and stir until slightly golden around the edges (about 30 seconds). Add crushed turmeric and cook and stir for about 1 minute. Add mushrooms and seitan (if using) and continue to cook and stir until everything is thoroughly tinted yellow by the turmeric (about 1 minute).

4. Stir in salt, sugar, stock powder, turmeric powder (if using), and ground pepper, and then remove from heat.

5. Transfer to a platter and garnish with cilantro or Vietnamese mint, crushed peanuts, and sliced chili pepper (if using).

NOTE *If fresh turmeric is unavailable in your location, you can replace it with the suggested amount of turmeric powder instead. However, be sure to only add the turmeric powder with the seasonings in step 4.*

LEMONGRASS CHILI TOFU

There are two different ways to make this dish (đậu phụ sả ớt): you can coat deep-fried tofu with fried lemongrass and chili peppers, or you can stuff it with lemongrass and chili peppers before you deep-fry it. I prefer the former (below) for weeknight meals, as it's much quicker and simpler to prepare. The latter method (see page 82) takes a bit more time and skill (especially for stuffing), but it's totally worth the effort for special occasions or when you want to impress someone.

SKILL LEVEL Moderate | **YIELD** 4 servings

COATED METHOD

28 ounces (794 g) firm tofu

2 tablespoons vegetable oil, plus more for deep frying

2 ounces (50 g) minced lemongrass

1 teaspoon minced bird's eye chili pepper

1 teaspoon vegetable or mushroom stock powder

½ teaspoon salt

1 teaspoon sugar

½ teaspoon turmeric powder

2 tablespoons soy sauce

1 bird's eye chili pepper, sliced on the bias, for garnish

2 or 3 sprigs of cilantro, for garnish

1 large cucumber, sliced, for serving

continued on following page

COATED METHOD

1. Cut tofu into cubes about 1 by 2 inches (2.5 by 5 cm).

2. Fill the bottom of a small or medium saucepan with about 1 inch (2.5 cm) of oil and heat over low heat. After about 3 minutes, check with a cooking thermometer to see if oil has reached 320°F (160°C). (You can also dip the pointy end of a wooden chopstick in the oil, and if a steady stream of bubbles appears around it, the oil is ready.) Carefully drop in tofu cubes, cooking in batches if necessary, and fry until golden brown (about 8 minutes).

3. With a slotted spoon, transfer tofu to a paper towel–lined plate to drain.

4. In a medium skillet, heat 2 tablespoons of oil over low heat. When hot, add lemongrass and chili pepper, and cook and stir until golden brown (1 to 2 minutes). Add stock powder, salt, sugar, and turmeric powder, and stir well.

5. Add fried tofu and drizzle with soy sauce. Toss until well-coated, and then remove from heat.

6. Arrange tofu on a platter, garnish with chili slices and cilantro, and serve with cucumber slices.

continued from previous page

STUFFED METHOD

2 tablespoons vegetable oil, plus more for deep-frying

2 ounces (50 g) minced lemongrass

1 tablespoon minced leek or scallion (white part only)

1 teaspoon minced bird's eye chili pepper

28 ounces (794 g) firm tofu

1 cup (240 ml) vegetable oil, for deep-frying

1 bird's eye chili pepper, sliced, for garnish

2 or 3 sprigs of cilantro, for garnish

1 large cucumber, sliced, for serving

3 tablespoons soy sauce, for serving

STUFFED METHOD

1. In a medium skillet, heat 2 tablespoons of oil over low heat. When hot, add lemongrass, leek, and chili pepper, and cook and stir until golden (about 2 minutes). Transfer to a bowl.

2. Cut tofu into 2 by 3-inch (5 by 7.5 cm) pieces that are ½ inch (1 cm) thick. Being careful not to cut all the way through, use a knife to slice into one side of each tofu piece and create space for the filling.

3. Stuff about 1 teaspoon of the filling into the created space of one of the tofu pieces. Repeat with the remaining tofu and filling.

4. Fill the bottom of a large skillet with about 1 inch (2.5 cm) of oil and heat over low heat. After about 3 minutes, check with a cooking thermometer to see if the oil has reached 320°F (160°C). (You can also dip the pointy end of a wooden chopstick in the oil, and if a steady stream of bubbles appears around it, the oil is ready.) Carefully drop in tofu and fry until golden brown on both sides (about 8 minutes). With a slotted spoon, transfer tofu to a paper towel–lined plate to drain.

5. Arrange tofu on a platter, garnish with chili slices and cilantro, and serve with cucumber slices and a bowl of soy sauce for dipping.

GRILLED MUSHROOMS WITH CRISPY GLUTINOUS PUFFS

Crispy glutinous puffs are delicious sticky rice cakes often served in Vietnam as an accompaniment to grilled chicken or roasted duck. You can also serve them solo or enjoy them as a snack. This recipe (nấm nướng xôi chiên phồng) turns them into mini buns with a grilled mushroom filling, which is also a great option for canapés.

SKILL LEVEL Advanced | **YIELD** 10 puffs

GLUTINOUS PUFFS

3½ ounces (100 g) peeled split mung beans, rinsed, soaked, and drained (page 11)

7 ounces (200 g) sticky rice, rinsed, soaked for 1 hour, and drained

¼ cup (50 g) sugar

½ cup (120 ml) full-fat, unsweetened coconut milk

¼ cup (50 g) water

¼ cup (60 ml) vegetable oil, plus more for deep-frying

FILLING

10½ ounces (300 g) king oyster mushrooms (see Note on page 84), rinsed with salted water

2 tablespoons vegetable oil, plus more for greasing

2 cloves garlic, minced, or 1 tablespoon minced leek (white part only)

1 tablespoon minced lemongrass

2 tablespoons soy sauce

1 tablespoon sugar

1 teaspoon sriracha sauce

Few sprigs cilantro, for garnish

1. MAKE THE GLUTINOUS PUFFS Combine the soaked mung beans and sticky rice in a colander and toss well.

2. In a small saucepan, heat ¼ cup (50 g) sugar and coconut milk over medium heat. Stir until sugar is completely dissolved, and then remove from heat.

3. Combine sticky rice, mung beans, coconut milk mixture, and water in a medium saucepan with a tight-fitting lid and stir. Bring to a boil and cook over medium heat until the water level drops below the surface of the beans and rice (about 5 minutes). Reduce heat to low, cover, and simmer for an additional 15 minutes without lifting the lid. Remove pot from heat and let sit for 5 minutes. Alternatively, you can combine all ingredients for the puffs in a rice cooker and press Start to cook.

4. While still hot, transfer the rice and beans to the greased bowl of a stand mixer. Attach the dough hook and knead on high speed, while gradually adding ¼ cup (60 ml) of vegetable oil. Knead until the rice and beans have broken down and a very smooth, thick, and sticky paste forms (about 10 minutes). Alternatively, transfer the rice and beans to a large, oiled metal bowl. Wearing rubber gloves, knead the mixture while it is still hot with your hands until a smooth, thick, and sticky paste forms (15 to 20 minutes).

5. Scrape down the sides of the bowl and transfer the paste to an oiled piece of plastic wrap large enough to enclose it. Using your hands, form the mixture into a cylinder about 2 inches (5 cm) in diameter and let cool.

6. Grease a knife with some vegetable oil, unwrap the rice and bean dough cylinder, and cut into ½-inch (1 cm) rounds. Roll out each round to reduce the thickness by half while keeping the shape.

continued on following page

continued from previous page

7. Fill the bottom of a medium saucepan with 2 inches (5 cm) of oil and place over medium-low heat. Heat oil to 320°F (160°C). (You can check the temperature with a cooking thermometer or insert one end of a chopstick in the oil; if bubbles appear around it, the oil is ready for deep-frying). Dip a spatula into the oil to prevent sticking, and then gently drop in 1 or 2 sticky rice patties (any more and you risk them sticking). Fry over medium-low heat until they float to the surface and the exterior is no longer sticky (1 to 2 minutes). To make them puffy, press them into the pan with the spatula one or two times per side. When golden brown on one side, flip, and repeat on the other. Use a wire spider or slotted spoon to transfer each sticky rice puff to a cooling rack to drain.

8. MAKE THE FILLIING Cut the king oyster mushrooms lengthwise into slices about ¼-inch (6 mm) thick. Lightly score a ¼-inch (6 mm) diamond pattern on the slices, put them on a large rimmed plate, and set aside.

9. In a small saucepan, heat 2 tablespoons of vegetable oil over medium-low heat. When hot, add garlic and lemongrass and cook and stir until slightly golden (about 1 minute). Reduce heat to low and add soy sauce and sugar. Simmer until sauce thickens (about 2 minutes), and then remove from heat and let cool.

10. With a rubber spatula, scrape all the marinade from the pan onto the mushroom plate. Use your fingers to coat the mushrooms thoroughly with the marinade and let them sit for 15 minutes.

11. After the 15 minutes, pour the excess marinade on the mushroom plate into a small saucepan and set aside.

12. Lightly coat an iron skillet or a pan with a heavy bottom with vegetable oil and place over high heat. When hot, add mushrooms and any marinade left on plate and cook until a noticeable brown crust forms (1 to 2 minutes per side). Use tongs to flip mushrooms.

13. Simmer the reserved marinade in the small saucepan over low heat until thickened (1 to 2 minutes), and then stir in sriracha.

14. To serve, assemble everything in the same order you would a burger: Place a glutinous puff on the bottom, followed by mushrooms, some cilantro, and a light drizzling of sauce. Top with a second glutinous puff, secure with a toothpick, and enjoy.

NOTE *When you're shopping for king oyster mushrooms, look for some that have firm, shiny caps and white stems, without any bruises or brown spots.*

SOUPS & NOODLES

While soup is usually served as part of a meal in Vietnam, that doesn't mean you can't make a big enough pot to feed everyone on a busy weeknight. Whether you are in the mood for sweet-and-sour, pumpkin and peanut, or sponge gourd and mushroom soup, these recipes will guide you through the prep, the seasoning, and the simmering. However, the main star of the show in this section is the famously delicious pho, and the recipe I've included is full of flavor.

PUMPKIN AND PEANUT SOUP

In Vietnam, soup is usually served with other dishes as part of the meal, rather than as an appetizer. You might be used to a more liquid-velvet texture in your pumpkin soup, but this recipe (canh bí đỏ đậu phộng) combines cubed pumpkin and chunky peanuts in a rich broth to create an incredibly unique flavor.

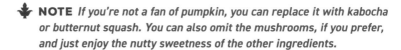

SKILL LEVEL Moderate | **YIELD** 4 servings

3½ ounces (100 g) mushrooms (straw, portobello, enoki, or white), stems trimmed and rinsed in salted water

1 tablespoon minced leek (white part only)

1 teaspoon vegetable or mushroom stock powder, plus more if needed

¼ teaspoon freshly ground black pepper

3 ounces (90 g) raw peanuts with skin, soaked in room-temperature water for a few hours

1 tablespoon vegetable oil

4 cups (1 L) water

1 teaspoon salt, plus more if needed

17½ ounces (500 g) pumpkin (see Note), peeled, seeds removed, and cut into 2-inch (5 cm) cubes

Few sprigs sawtooth herb or cilantro, finely chopped, for garnish

1. Cut smaller mushrooms in half and larger ones into quarters.

2. In a small bowl, combine mushrooms, minced leek, stock powder, and pepper. Mix well and set aside for about 15 minutes.

3. Remove the silky skin of the raw peanuts and roughly crush them with a mortar and pestle. (Alternatively, you can put them in a resealable plastic bag and crush them with a rolling pin).

4. In a medium saucepan, heat oil over medium heat. Add the mushroom-leek mixture and cook and stir until tender (2 to 3 minutes). Transfer contents of saucepan to a bowl.

5. Add the water to the same saucepan, along with salt and peanuts, and cook, occasionally skimming off foam, until the peanuts are quite soft (about 15 minutes).

6. Add pumpkin cubes, cover, and cook over low heat until soft (about 15 minutes more). When you can easily break the cubes with a chopstick or fork, they are done.

7. Return the mushroom-leek mixture to the soup and season with salt and/or stock powder to taste.

8. Garnish with sawtooth herb or cilantro and serve hot.

NOTE *If you're not a fan of pumpkin, you can replace it with kabocha or butternut squash. You can also omit the mushrooms, if you prefer, and just enjoy the nutty sweetness of the other ingredients.*

THAI-STYLE SWEET-AND-SOUR SOUP

Infused with classic Thai herbs, such as lemongrass and makrut lime leaves, this tamarind- and tomato-based soup (canh chua kiểu Thái) is the perfect blend of sweet, sour, and savory. It's a tasty way to rejuvenate your dinner menu, and everyone is sure to love it!

SKILL LEVEL Moderate | **YIELD** 4 servings

1 ounce (28 g) tamarind pulps (page 17; see Note), seeds removed

¼ cup (60 ml) hot water

2 to 3 lemongrass stalks

5 ounces (142 g) firm tofu

2 tablespoons vegetable oil

1 tablespoon minced leek (white part only)

5 ounces (142 g) plum tomatoes, cut into wedges

½ teaspoon salt, plus more if needed

1 teaspoon vegetable or mushroom stock powder

1 tablespoon sugar

4 or 5 makrut lime leaves, roughly torn into chunks, center stems removed

1 tablespoon (or to taste) vegan fish sauce (page 20) (optional)

3½ ounces (100 g) straw or white button mushrooms, rinsed in salted water and halved

3½ ounces (100 g) enoki mushrooms, stems trimmed and rinsed in salted water

1. Soak tamarind pulps in the hot water for about 15 minutes. Use a spoon to break up the pulps, press through a strainer to get a tamarind paste, and then discard the fibrous part. Set aside.

2. Trim off the green upper parts and lowest, toughest portions at the bases of the lemongrass stalks. Place on a cutting board and bruise the bulbous end with a pestle or meat tenderizer to release fragrance and flavor.

3. Cut tofu into 1-inch (2.5 cm) cubes and set aside.

4. Heat oil in a 2-quart (2 L) saucepan over medium-low heat. When hot, add the leeks and cook and stir until fragrant (about 30 seconds). Add lemongrass stalks, tomatoes, 4 cups (1 L) of water, salt, stock powder, sugar, and lime leaves to the pan and bring to a boil.

5. Stir in tamarind paste and tofu, and season with vegan fish sauce (if using) or more salt. Continue to boil until the tomatoes are tender (3 to 5 minutes). During the last minute of cooking, separate the mushrooms into bite-size bunches and stir them in. When soup returns to a boil, remove from heat.

6. Transfer soup to bowls and serve hot.

 NOTE *Unfortunately, tamarind can be difficult to find in many areas, but you might be able to find the paste or concentrate at your local Asian grocery store or online. For this recipe, use 2 tablespoons of tamarind paste or 2 teaspoons of tamarind concentrate mixed with 4 teaspoons of water.*

VEGAN CRAB SOUP

Canh riêu is a classic Vietnamese soup made from pounded seafood
(rice paddy crab, shrimp, or fish) and a stock base of tomato. In this version,
you'll use tofu crumbles and minced mushrooms as your protein substitutions.
The cilantro and annatto oil create a similar flavor and color to the original dish.

SKILL LEVEL Moderate | **YIELD** 4 servings

5½ ounces (150 g) firm tofu, finely crumbled with a fork

5½ ounces (150 g) silken tofu, finely crumbled with a fork

2 teaspoons vegetable or mushroom stock powder, divided

½ teaspoon salt, plus more if needed

½ teaspoon sugar

1 cube store-bought or homemade chao (page 22), finely crushed

1 tablespoon fermented soybean sauce

1 tablespoon annatto oil (page 26)

½ teaspoon freshly ground black pepper

2 tablespoons vegetable oil, divided

1 tablespoon minced leek (white part only)

2 plum tomatoes, cubed

4 cups (1 L) water

3½ ounces (100 g) minced enoki mushrooms, stems trimmed and rinsed with salted water

1 ounce (28 g) sawtooth herb or cilantro, finely chopped, for garnish

1. In a large bowl, combine both types of tofu, 1 teaspoon of the stock powder, salt, sugar, chao, fermented soybean sauce, annatto oil, and pepper, and mix well. Cover and let sit for 15 minutes to allow the flavor to develop.

2. In a medium skillet, heat 1 tablespoon of the vegetable oil over low heat. When hot, add leek and cook and stir until fragrant (about 1 minute). Add the tofu mixture and flatten its surface with a spatula. Cook on low until the mixture is set (2 to 3 more minutes), and then remove from heat.

3. In a medium saucepan, heat the remaining 1 tablespoon vegetable oil over medium heat. Add tomatoes and cook and stir until soft (about 3 minutes). Add water and bring to a boil.

4. Add mushrooms and the remaining 1 teaspoon stock powder, taste, and add more salt if needed. Cook over medium heat until tomatoes are broken down and mushrooms are soft (about 2 more minutes), and then remove from heat.

5. Transfer to a large serving bowl or divide into smaller serving bowls.

6. Add the tofu mixture (riêu) to the hot soup, garnish with sawtooth herb or cilantro, and serve hot.

SWEET-AND-SOUR SOUP WITH SEAWEED

Beloved for its tomato- and pineapple-flavored broth and fresh herbal garnish, canh chua is an iconic Vietnamese sweet-and-sour soup. While the traditional version is cooked with fish, this plant-based version calls for dried wakame or dulse seaweed to add that hint of the ocean. Wakame is commonly used in Japanese miso soup and has a briny, subtly sweet flavor. Dulse comes in purplish-red flakes that have a nutty, peppery flavor with a chewy texture. To rehydrate either type of seaweed, place it in a bowl and cover with cool water for a few minutes.

SKILL LEVEL Moderate | **YIELD** 3 or 4 servings

1 tablespoon vegetable oil

1 tablespoon minced leek
(white part only)

3½ ounces (100 g) enoki mushrooms
(see Note), rinsed with salted water
and separated into bite-size bundles

3½ ounces (100 g) fresh pineapple,
cut into triangular slices

1 medium plum tomato, cut
into wedges

1 teaspoon salt, divided

1 tablespoon tamarind paste or
1 teaspoon tamarind concentrate
mixed with 2 teaspoons water

6 cups (1.5 L) water

7 okras, sliced crosswise on the bias

1 teaspoon vegetable or mushroom
stock powder

1 ounce (28 g) dried seaweed
(wakame or dulse; see Note),
soaked and roughly chopped

7 ounces (200 g) silken tofu, cut
into 1-inch (2.5 cm) cubes

2 ounces (56 g) rice paddy herb,
chopped

2 ounces (56 g) cilantro, chopped

1 bird's eye chili pepper, sliced,
for garnish (optional)

1. In a large saucepan, heat oil over medium-low heat. When hot, add leek and cook and stir until fragrant (about 1 minute). Add mushrooms, pineapple, tomato, and ½ teaspoon of the salt, and stir well.

2. Add tamarind paste and the water, and bring to a boil over high heat. Add okra, stock powder, remaining ½ teaspoon of salt, seaweed, and tofu, and bring to a boil again.

3. Add rice paddy herb and cilantro, and cook for 1 more minute only (overcooked seaweed tends to develop an overly fishy taste and lose its color and crunchiness). Remove from heat.

4. Garnish with chili slices (if using) and serve hot.

🌿 **NOTE** *You should be able to find both types of seaweed in the dried pantry aisle in most Asian grocery stores or the Asian section at most supermarkets.*

SPONGE GOURD AND MUSHROOM SOUP

This soup (canh mướp nấm hương) is a must-try, especially for hot summer days. Sponge gourd is an oblong fruit with green skin when it's young. It also sometimes has ridges or ridge lines on its skin. It is harvested young, when the interior is a smooth, creamy white and has a mild, but sweet, zucchini-like taste. If you have trouble finding sponge gourd locally, you can use ridge gourd or zucchini instead.

SKILL LEVEL Basic | **YIELD** 4 servings

1¾ ounces (50 g) dried shiitake mushrooms, soaked (page 12)

1 tablespoon minced leek (white part only)

1½ teaspoons vegetable or mushroom stock powder, divided

1 teaspoon soy sauce

¼ teaspoon freshly ground black pepper

1 tablespoon vegetable oil

4 cups (1 L) water

3½ ounces (100 g) sweet leaf bush (see Note) or spinach, stems removed and washed (optional)

10½ ounces (300 g) sponge gourd, ridge gourd, or zucchini, peeled and cut along the grain into half-moon slices

1. Cut the rehydrated shiitake mushrooms into strips and set aside.

2. In a small bowl, combine the leek, ½ teaspoon of the stock powder, soy sauce, and pepper. Mix well and set aside for 15 minutes.

3. Heat the oil in a small saucepan over medium-low heat. When hot, add the leek mixture and cook and stir until fragrant (about 30 seconds). Add mushrooms and cook and stir until tender (about 2 minutes).

4. Add the water to a medium saucepan and bring to a boil over medium-high heat. Add sweet leaf bush (if using), sponge gourd, and the remaining 1 teaspoon stock powder. Let soup boil for 2 minutes longer, or until sponge gourd is soft and silky and sweet leaf bush is tender. Remove from heat.

5. Transfer to bowls and serve hot.

 NOTE *Sweet leaf bush is extremely difficult to find in cooler climates. If you can't get your hands on any, you can either omit it or replace it with spinach.*

PHO

Originating from the Nam Dinh Province southeast of Hanoi in the early twentieth century, phở is one of the most famous traditional dishes in Vietnam. In fact, this is often the dish that introduces most people to Vietnamese cuisine.

SKILL LEVEL Advanced | **YIELD** 8 to 10 servings

BROTH

16 cups (4 L) water

1 medium juicy red or Gala apple, peeled and cut into 2-inch (5 cm) cubes

1 medium Asian or Bosc pear, peeled and cut into 2-inch (5 cm) cubes

2 medium carrots, peeled and sliced into 1-inch (2.5 cm) thick rounds

1 kohlrabi, chayote, or daikon radish, peeled and cut into 2-inch (5 cm) cubes

1 medium yellow onion, peeled

2 ounces (50 g) rock sugar

2 to 3 tablespoons salt

AROMA

2 Asian shallots or 1 medium yellow onion

2 pieces (2 ounces/55 g) ginger, thinly sliced

3 star anise

2 cinnamon sticks

2 black cardamom pods (see Note on page 100)

Salt, to taste

Vegetable or mushroom stock powder, to taste

continued on following page

1. TO MAKE THE BROTH Fill a large stockpot with the water, and add the apple, pear, carrot, kohlrabi, onion, rock sugar, and 2 to 3 tablespoons of salt. Bring to a boil, and then reduce heat to low. Simmer uncovered until the fruits and vegetables are tender (about 30 minutes).

2. CREATE THE AROMA Heat the shallots and ginger slices directly over an open flame on the stove until slightly charred on all sides. Toast the star anise, cinnamon sticks, and cardamom pods in a small skillet over medium-low heat for 2 to 3 minutes, until fragrant.

3. Peel the shallots, and then rinse with the ginger under warm running water. Scrape off all charred bits and place in large tea bags or wrap securely in cheesecloth with star anise, cinnamon sticks, and black cardamom. Add to stockpot, and then season broth with salt and stock powder.

4. MAKE THE TOPPINGS In a small skillet, heat ¼ cup (60 ml) of the oil over medium-low heat. Once hot, add the tofu and cook until golden brown on all sides (10 to 15 minutes). Transfer the tofu to a cooling rack or paper towel–lined plate to drain. Once cool, cut the fried tofu and soaked bean curd into bite-size pieces.

5. Combine the fried tofu and bean curd slices in a large bowl and season with ½ teaspoon of the salt, ½ tablespoon of the granulated sugar, 1 teaspoon of the stock powder, ½ teaspoon of the five-spice powder, and 1 tablespoon of the soy sauce.

6. In a separate large bowl, combine the mushrooms and season with the remaining ½ teaspoon salt, ½ tablespoon granulated sugar, 1 teaspoon stock powder, ½ teaspoon five-spice powder, and 1 tablespoon soy sauce.

7. Heat 1 tablespoon of the vegetable oil in a large skillet over medium-low heat. When hot, add half of the minced leek, and cook and stir until fragrant (about 1 minute). Add the tofu–bean curd mixture and cook and stir until seasonings are well absorbed (about 3 minutes). Transfer to a clean bowl.

8. Return skillet to medium-low heat and add remaining 1 tablespoon vegetable oil. Add remaining leek and cook and stir until fragrant (about 1 minute). Add mushroom mixture and cook and stir until soft and seasonings are well absorbed (about 3 minutes). Transfer to a separate clean bowl.

continued from previous page

TOPPINGS

¼ cup (60 ml) plus 2 tablespoons vegetable oil, divided

1 block (14 ounces/400 g) firm tofu, drained

3½ ounces (100 g) dried bean curd stick or sheet, soaked (page 10), or dried mock beef slices, soaked (page 10)

1 teaspoon salt, divided

1 tablespoon granulated sugar, divided

2 teaspoons vegetable or mushroom stock powder, divided

1 teaspoon five-spice powder, divided

2 tablespoons soy sauce, divided

9 ounces (250 g) fresh mushrooms (straw, king oyster, or shiitake), stems trimmed and sliced

1 tablespoon minced leek (white part only)

FOR SERVING

16 ounces (454 g) dried flat rice noodles or 2¼ pounds (1 kg) fresh pho noodles

2 ounces (56 g) sawtooth herb, chopped

3½ ounces (100 g) Asian basil

1 pound (454 g) mung bean sprouts, blanched

1 lime, cut into wedges

1 bird's eye chili pepper, sliced

¼ cup (60 ml) sriracha sauce (optional)

¼ cup (60 ml) hoisin sauce (optional)

9. FOR SERVING Follow the instructions on the package to cook the dried noodles.

10. Fill each serving bowl about one-third with noodles, add tofu and mushroom toppings, top with sawtooth herb, and then ladle the hot broth over the top.

11. Serve with a platter of fresh herbs, blanched mung bean sprouts, lime wedges, and sliced chili peppers, along with sriracha (if using) and hoisin sauce (if using).

 NOTE *Black cardamom is larger than green cardamom, has a smoky flavor, and is mostly used in savory dishes. If you have trouble finding black, you can substitute with green, but your pho will lack that signature smoky, hot flavor.*

PHO BROTH COOKING TIPS

The broth is considered to be the soul of pho. However, when it comes to the vegan version, not everyone knows how to combine and prep their vegetables properly. Below are a few tips that will help you create a delicious (and nutritious) broth:

- **COMBINE MORE VARIETIES OF FRUITS AND VEGETABLES** This creates a more delicious, richer flavor than you get when using just one type. In addition to apples, pears, carrots, and kohlrabi, you can also add onion, celery, leek tops, parsnips, chayote, daikon, and more. Limit starchier vegetables, like potatoes and sweet potatoes, as they tend to turn a broth cloudy when simmered for long stretches.

- **CUT ALL VEGETABLES ROUGHLY THE SAME SIZE** This ensures they have similar surface areas to absorb the water. About 1 to 2 inches (2.5 to 5 cm) is generally good.

- **USE THE SKINS AND ROOTS** The ends and skins of onions, carrots, parsnips, and other veggies can be included in your broth.

- **GRILL OR PREBAKE THE VEGGIES** Just toss them on a baking sheet and bake at 400°F (200°C) for 15 minutes before you cook the broth.

- **ADD MUSHROOMS WHENEVER YOU'RE AFTER A SAVORY FLAVOR** They're rich in umami (amino acids and nucleotides) and will give your broth that "meaty" flavor without any meat. I prefer dried shiitake mushrooms, but feel free to use your favorite or mix different kinds.

- **ADD FRUIT WHEN YOU NEED SOMETHING SWEET** Apples and pears, in particular, add an all-natural sweetness to a broth. You can also use sugarcane or kombu, a type of kelp used often in Japanese cuisine.

- **ADD ENOUGH WATER** A good ratio is 16 cups (4 L) of water for every 2 to 4½ pounds (1 to 2 kg) of vegetables. Always cook them in cold water, so the overly sweet flavors are extracted at the right temperature.

- **BATCH-COOK YOUR BROTH** You can make a large amount of broth ahead of time so that it will be ready to warm up whenever you need it. Store in an airtight container in the refrigerator for up to 1 week or in the freezer for up to 2 months.

QUANG NOODLES

Mì Quảng noodles are a specialty from the Quang Nam Province and Da Nang city in Central Vietnam, which also happens to be where I'm from. This half-noodle, half-salad dish is the ultimate comfort food. Unlike other noodle soups, fresh greens are part of this dish, not optional add-ins. Although we use a lot less of it for each serving, the broth should also be saltier than a normal soup, yet not as salty as a sauce. Every cook has their own variation of mì Quảng. In fact, this is my mom's recipe, who I believe makes the best mì Quảng in the world! Mì Quảng is known for its wide, vibrant yellow turmeric noodles; however, you can use flat, wide white rice noodles (sợi mì Quảng).

SKILL LEVEL Moderate | **YIELD** 8 to 10 servings

6 cups (1.5 L) water

12½ ounces (350 g) pumpkin, peeled and cut into cubes

9 ounces (250 g) chayote or kohlrabi, peeled and half cubed and half diced

7 ounces (200 g) taro (page 17), diced

2½ teaspoons salt, divided

½ cup (120 ml) cold-pressed peanut or vegetable oil, divided

1 block (14 ounces/400 g) firm tofu, cut into 1-inch (2.5 cm) thick steaks

2 finger-size pieces fresh turmeric (see Note on page 102), peeled and roughly chopped

2 ounces (56 g) leek (white and green parts separated), roughly chopped, divided

3½ ounces (100 g) mushrooms (straw, shiitake, or similar), cut into bite-size pieces

4¼ ounces (120 g) store-bought or homemade seitan (page 12), sliced

1 teaspoon vegetable or mushroom stock powder

1 teaspoon sugar

½ teaspoon freshly ground black pepper

1. Add the water to a medium saucepan and bring to a boil over medium-high heat. Add pumpkin and chayote cubes, cook until fork-tender (about 15 minutes), and then remove from heat. Purée the mixture with a hand blender. Add diced chayote and taro to saucepan with 1 teaspoon of the salt and cook over medium heat until fork-tender (about 7 minutes).

2. Heat ¼ cup (60 ml) of the oil in a small skillet over medium-low heat. When hot, add tofu steaks and cook until golden brown on all sides (10 to 15 minutes). Transfer to a cooling rack or paper towel–lined plate to drain.

3. If using fresh turmeric, place it in a resealable plastic bag and crush it with a pestle (avoid using the mortar, as the turmeric may stain it and/or your hands) or meat tenderizer.

4. In a mortar and pestle, finely crush the white part of the leek with ½ teaspoon of the salt.

5. In a medium skillet, heat the remaining ¼ cup (60 ml) oil over medium-low heat. When hot, add leek and cook and stir until golden (about 2 minutes). If using fresh turmeric, add and quickly cook it for about 10 seconds.

6. Add mushrooms, tofu, and seitan to the skillet. Season with turmeric powder (if using), remaining 1 teaspoon salt, stock powder, and sugar. Toss well, cook over low heat until mushrooms are tender (2 to 3 minutes), and then turn off heat. Add green part of leek and ground pepper.

continued on following page

continued from previous page

16 ounces (454 g) dried flat rice noodles or 2¼ pounds (1 kg) fresh mì Quảng or flat rice noodles

10½ ounces (300 g) leaf or iceberg lettuce, shredded or torn

3½ ounces (100 g) fresh green herbs (such as mint, perilla, cilantro, and/or Asian basil leaves), chopped

2 sesame rice crackers

1 ounce (28 g) cilantro, chopped, for garnish

½ cup (72 g) crushed roasted peanuts, for garnish

2 limes, cut into wedges, for serving

5 whole green serrano chili peppers, for serving

3½ ounces (100 g) banana blossom, prepped and shredded (page 15)

7. Follow the directions on the package to cook the dried flat rice noodles. If using fresh noodles, quickly blanch them in hot water if they have been refrigerated.

8. Fill serving bowls halfway with noodles, and then ladle soup over the top until it barely covers them. Add some lettuce and herbs to each bowl. Break a rice cracker into small pieces and add to bowl. Garnish with cilantro, crushed peanuts, and a full piece of sesame rice cracker.

9. Squeeze lime wedges over the top of the bowls and mix well. Serve with serrano chili peppers, banana blossom, and more lettuce and herbs.

 NOTE *Turmeric is one of the key ingredients as it creates the special flavor of this dish. Fresh is best, but if it's not available in your area, you can use 1 teaspoon of powdered turmeric*

QUANG NOODLE SALAD

This version of Quang-style noodles (mì Quảng chay trộn) is made without the broth, so it's easier to prepare than the traditional version (page 101). I recommend using enoki, oyster, and/or white beech mushrooms to create the best possible sauce.

SKILL LEVEL Moderate | **YIELD** 4 servings

¼ cup (60 ml) plus 3 tablespoons vegetable oil, divided

1 block (14 ounces/400 g) firm tofu

1 ounce (28 g) dried bean curd sheet, soaked (page 10) and cut into 4-inch (10 cm) squares (optional)

1 tablespoon minced leek (white part only)

7 ounces (200 g) fresh mushrooms (enoki, oyster, white beech, or similar), stems trimmed and separated

¾ ounce (20 g) dried wood ear mushrooms, soaked (page 13) and thinly sliced

¾ ounce (20 g) dried shiitake mushrooms, soaked (page 12) and thinly sliced

1 tablespoon soy sauce, plus more to taste if needed

1 tablespoon vegetarian oyster sauce

1 teaspoon vegetable or mushroom stock powder

½ teaspoon sugar

10 ounces (283 g) dried flat rice noodles or 21 ounces (600 g) fresh mì Quảng or flat rice noodles

3½ ounces (100 g) mung bean sprouts

3½ ounces (100 g) green cabbage, shredded

1 ounce (28 g) round leaf mint or mint, roughly chopped if leaves are large

10 perilla leaves, chopped

1 green chili pepper (serrano or jalapeño), sliced

3 tablespoons crushed roasted peanuts, for garnish

1. Heat ¼ cup (60 ml) of the oil in a small saucepan over medium-low heat. When hot, add the tofu and cook until golden brown on all sides (10 to 15 minutes). Transfer to a cooling rack or paper towel–lined plate to drain. When cool, cut into bite-size pieces.

2. Drop the dried bean curd (if using) into the remaining oil, cook until they puff up (5 to 10 seconds), and then immediately remove from oil with tongs and place on a cooling rack to drain excess oil.

3. In a large skillet, heat remaining 3 tablespoons vegetable oil over medium-low heat. When hot, add leek and cook and stir until slightly golden (about 1 minute). Transfer half of the fried leek oil to a small bowl and reserve for later.

4. Add all mushrooms, soy sauce, vegetarian oyster sauce, stock powder, and sugar to the remaining oil in the skillet. Cook and stir until mushrooms are tender and browned (4 to 5 minutes), and then add tofu. Cook and stir for about 30 seconds, and then remove pan from heat and set aside to cool.

5. Follow the directions on the package to cook the dried flat rice noodles.

6. In a large bowl, combine the cooked noodles with cooked mushrooms and tofu, along with juices from the skillet. Add the bean sprouts, cabbage, mint, perilla leaves, chili pepper, and reserved leek oil. Mix well and add more soy sauce to taste if needed.

7. Transfer salad to a platter, garnish with peanuts and fried bean curd (if using), and serve.

VEGAN CRAB NOODLE SOUP

Originating in the northern region of Vietnam, bún riêu is now a common breakfast all over the country. For this recipe, you'll use a seasoned, mashed tofu instead of rice paddy crabs, along with chao and fermented soybean sauce. You can either stir the sauce into the broth during the last step or set it out as a condiment.

SKILL LEVEL Moderate | **YIELD** 4 servings

RIÊU

1 block (14 ounces/400 g) firm tofu, mashed

1 tablespoon sugar

1 teaspoon vegetable or mushroom stock powder, plus more to taste

4 teaspoons annatto oil (page 26), divided

BROTH

1 cup (120 ml) vegetable oil, divided

8 ounces (227 g) firm tofu, cut into 1-inch (2.5 cm) cubes

1 tablespoon minced leek (white part only)

7 ounces (200 g) plum tomatoes, cubed

3½ ounces (100 g) fresh mushrooms (straw, beech, or king oyster), stems trimmed and sliced

5 cups (1.2 L) vegetable broth, store-bought or homemade (page 99)

1 teaspoon salt, plus more if needed

1 teaspoon vegetable or mushroom stock powder, plus more if needed

1 tablespoon tamarind paste or 1 teaspoon tamarind concentrate mixed with 2 teaspoons water

1 tablespoon sugar

2 cubes store-bought or homemade chao (page 22) (optional)

2 tablespoons fermented soybean sauce (optional)

2 tablespoons water

10 ounces (283 g) dried rice vermicelli noodles

3½ ounces (100 g) leaf or iceberg lettuce, leaves torn into small pieces or shredded, for serving

3 ounces (90 g) perilla leaves, shredded, for serving

½ lime, cut into wedges, for serving

1. MAKE THE RIÊU In a medium bowl, combine mashed tofu, 1 tablespoon of sugar, 1 teaspoon of stock powder, and 2 teaspoons of the annatto oil, and mix well.

2. Heat the remaining 2 teaspoons annatto oil in a large skillet over medium-low heat. When hot, add tofu mixture, stir, and cook until tofu absorbs all seasoning (about 3 minutes). Transfer to a bowl and set aside.

3. MAKE THE BROTH Heat ½ cup (120 ml) of the vegetable oil in a medium nonstick skillet over medium-low heat. Add tofu cubes and cook until golden brown on all sides (10 to 15 minutes). Transfer to a cooling rack or paper towel–lined plate to drain.

4. In a medium stockpot, heat remaining ½ cup (120 ml) vegetable oil over medium-low heat. When hot, add leek and cook and stir until fragrant (about 1 minute). Add tomatoes and mushrooms, stir, and cook until soft (about 3 minutes). Add vegetable broth, salt, and stock powder.

5. Add tamarind paste, deep-fried tofu, and 1 tablespoon of sugar and bring to a boil. Cook over medium-low heat for 5 minutes. Season to taste with more salt and/or stock powder if needed.

6. If using, place chao and fermented soybean sauce in a food processor or blender and process with the water until smooth. (You can also mash by hand with a spoon.) Stir mixture into broth.

7. Follow the instructions on the package to cook the dried rice vermicelli noodles.

8. Divide the cooked noodles into serving bowls, spoon the riêu on top, and then ladle the hot broth over the top. Serve with a platter of shredded lettuce and perilla leaves with lime wedges on the side.

HỦ TIẾU

Hủ tiếu comes from Southwestern Vietnam and is widely served at the floating markets in the Mekong Delta. It is influenced by a Chinese-Cambodian dish called kuy teav. The original dish features chewy tapioca noodles, a pork- and daikon-based broth, and various toppings, including shrimp, squid, pork, quail eggs, garlic chives, and more. Dried hủ tiếu dai noodles are the best choice for this soup. They're slender sticks made mostly from tapioca. When cooked, they become translucent and tender, and they also retain the flavor of broth very well. I recommend cooking them in serving-size batches in a noodle strainer, rather than cooking them all at once, to avoid the noodles clumping together.

SKILL LEVEL Advanced | **YIELD** 8 to 10 servings

16 cups (4 L) water

1 medium red or Gala apple, peeled and cut into 2-inch (5 cm) cubes

1 medium Asian or Bosc pear, peeled and cut into 2-inch (5 cm) cubes

2 corncobs, cut into 1-inch (2.5 cm) rounds

10½ ounces (300 g) daikon radish, cut into 1-inch (2.5 cm) rounds

1 ounce (28 g) rock sugar

1 tablespoon salt, plus more to taste

1 teaspoon vegetable or mushroom stock powder, plus more to taste

¼ cup (60 ml) plus 5 tablespoons vegetable oil, divided

1 block (14 ounces/400 g) firm tofu

1 ounce (28 g) dried bean curd sheet, soaked (page 10) and cut into 4-inch (10 cm) square pieces (optional)

2 tablespoons minced leek (white part only)

2 tablespoons minced garlic

1½ ounces (32 g) salted preserved radish (see Note on page 110), soaked for 10 minutes, drained, and finely chopped (optional)

1 teaspoon granulated sugar

continued on following page

1. In a large stockpot, combine the water, apple, pear, corncobs, daikon radish, rock sugar, and 1 tablespoon of salt. Bring to a boil over high heat, and then reduce heat to medium-low. Allow to simmer for 1 hour. Taste the broth, and then season with more salt and/or stock powder if needed.

2. Heat ¼ cup (60 ml) of the oil in a small skillet over medium-low heat. When hot, add tofu and cook until golden brown on all sides (10 to 15 minutes). Transfer to a cooling rack or paper towel–lined plate to drain. When cool, cut tofu into bite-size slices.

3. Drop the dried bean curd (if using) into the remaining hot oil in the pan and cook until they puff up (5 to 10 seconds). Using tongs, remove immediately from oil and place on a cooling rack to drain.

4. In a medium skillet, heat 3 tablespoons of the oil over medium-low heat. When hot, add leek and cook and stir until golden brown (1 to 2 minutes). Using a slotted spoon, transfer to a small bowl.

5. Add garlic to the remaining oil in the pan and cook and stir over low heat until golden brown (about 30 seconds). Using a slotted spoon, transfer to a separate small bowl.

6. Add the chopped preserved radish (if using) to the remaining oil in the pan and cook and stir over low heat for 1 minute. Stir in granulated sugar, and then transfer to a third small bowl.

continued from previous page

10½ ounces (300 g) mushrooms (straw, king oyster, shiitake, or similar), stems trimmed and sliced

2 tablespoons soy sauce or vegan fish sauce (page 20)

Freshly ground black pepper, to taste

16 ounces (454 g) dried hủ tiếu dai noodles or dried flat rice noodles

7 ounces (200 g) fresh mung bean sprouts, blanched

1 ounce (28 g) cilantro, chopped, for garnish

3 bird's eye chili peppers, sliced, for garnish

7. Heat the remaining 2 tablespoons oil in the skillet over medium-low heat. Add mushrooms, soy sauce, and 1 teaspoon of stock powder. Cook and stir until mushrooms start to release moisture (about 1 minute), and then add fried tofu to absorb juices. Season to taste with salt, ground pepper, and more stock powder.

8. Place dried hủ tiếu noodles in a large bowl and cover with room-temperature water. Let soak for 15 minutes until softened, and then drain.

9. Bring a large saucepan of water to a boil over high heat and add mung bean sprouts. Blanch for 30 seconds, and then, using a wire spider or slotted spoon, transfer to a plate.

10. Add a handful of noodles to a noodle strainer, submerge in the boiling water the mung bean sprouts were blanched in, and cook until al dente (3 to 5 minutes). Repeat with remaining noodles. If using flat rice noodles, follow the instructions on the package.

11. Divide noodles and mung bean sprouts into serving bowls and top with mushroom-tofu mixture, fried leek and garlic, and sautéed preserved radish. Ladle the broth over the top, garnish with chopped cilantro, sliced chili peppers, and fried bean curd (if using), and serve hot.

 NOTE *Salted preserved radish is an umami-laden ingredient that helps amp up the flavor and crunchy texture of this dish. You can usually find it shredded and sold in packs in the dried foods aisle of any Asian grocery store.*

THICK NOODLE SOUP

This soup is called bánh canh in Vietnam: *bánh* is a generic term that refers to foods made from flour and/or starchy ingredients and *canh* means "soup." The traditional version of bánh canh is often made with crabs, pork hock, fish cakes, and/or shrimp. In this version, vegetables, fried tofu, and sponge gourd add flavor.

SKILL LEVEL Advanced | **YIELD** 1 (13½-ounce/400-ml) jar

BROTH

12 cups (3 L) water

1 medium chayote, peeled and cut into 1½-inch (4 cm) cubes

1 medium carrot, peeled and cut into 1½-inch (4 cm) cubes

½ daikon radish (about 4 inches/10 cm), cut into 1-inch (2.5 cm) rounds

1 medium corncob, cut into 1-inch (2.5 cm) rounds

1 teaspoon salt

NOODLES

1 package (15 ounces/425 g) fresh bánh canh noodles (see Note on page 112)

OR (make your own noodles) 2 cups (320 g) rice flour, plus more for dusting

2 cups (310 g) tapioca starch

1 teaspoon salt

2 cups (480 ml) boiling water

1 tablespoon vegetable oil

TOPPINGS

¼ cup (60 ml) vegetable oil

1 block (14 ounces/400 g) firm tofu

continued on following page

1. MAKE THE BROTH Add the water, chayote, carrot, daikon radish, corn, and 1 teaspoon of salt to a large saucepan, and bring to a boil over high heat. Reduce heat to medium-low and simmer until vegetables have lost their sweet flavor (about 1 hour).

2. MAKE THE NOODLES If using store-bought noodles, simply follow the directions on the package. To make your own, combine the rice flour, tapioca starch, and 1 teaspoon of salt in a large bowl. Make a hole in the center, carefully pour in boiling water, and mix with a spatula until water is fully incorporated (3 to 5 minutes).

3. When it is cool enough to handle, either knead the dough in a stand mixer using a dough hook for 10 minutes on medium speed or with your hands until it is soft and non-sticky. Cover with plastic wrap and let rest for about 30 minutes.

4. Sprinkle some flour on a work surface and, using a rolling pin, roll out the dough until it is about ¼ inch (6 mm) thick. Cut into 3-inch (7.5 cm) noodle strips.

5. Fill a large saucepan halfway with water and bring to a boil over high heat. Add 1 tablespoon of vegetable oil and the homemade noodles and cook until al dente and the noodles float to the surface (about 5 minutes). Dump into a colander and rinse under cold water to remove excess starch.

6. MAKE THE TOPPINGS Heat ¼ cup (60 mL) of vegetable oil in a small skillet over medium-low heat. When hot, add the tofu and cook until golden brown on all sides (10 to 15 minutes). Transfer the tofu to a cooling rack or paper towel–lined plate to drain. When cool, cut into ½-inch (1 cm) thick slices.

continued from previous page

3 tablespoons annatto oil (page 26)

2 ounces (56 g) chopped leek (white part only)

10½ ounces (300 g) mushrooms (shiitake, straw, white beech, or similar), stems trimmed and sliced

10½ ounces (300 g) sponge gourd (page 96), peeled and cut into half-moon slices

2 tablespoons vegan fish sauce (page 20) or soy sauce

1 ounce (28 g) Vietnamese mint, finely chopped, for garnish

1 teaspoon freshly ground black pepper, for garnish

7. In a medium skillet, heat annatto oil over medium-low heat. When hot, add leek and cook and stir until fragrant and slightly golden (about 1 minute). Add mushrooms, sponge gourd, and fried tofu slices. Season with vegan fish sauce and cook and stir until mushrooms and sponge gourd are tender (about 3 minutes). Remove from heat.

8. Fill a large serving bowl halfway with cooked noodles and top with tofu, mushrooms, and sponge gourd. Ladle hot broth over the top and garnish with chopped Vietnamese mint and ground pepper.

 NOTE *Bánh canh noodles are cut out of a thick sheet of dough and can be made from tapioca, wheat, or rice flour, or a combination of those. If you'd rather not make your own noodles, you can buy fresh bánh canh, Japanese udon, or Chinese cu mian noodles at your local Asian grocery store.*

GRILLED SEITAN VERMICELLI NOODLE SALAD

The vegan version of this famous dish (bún mì căn nướng) calls for seitan (wheat gluten) instead of pork. This salad is perfect on hot summer days when you want something satisfying and refreshing.

SKILL LEVEL Moderate | **YIELD** 4 servings

SALAD

7 ounces (200 g) store-bought or homemade seitan (page 12), cut into thin slices

½ teaspoon five-spice powder

1 tablespoon minced lemongrass

1 teaspoon sugar

½ teaspoon vegetable or mushroom stock powder

¼ teaspoon freshly ground black pepper

1 tablespoon vegetable oil

1 tablespoon soy sauce

1 tablespoon vegetarian oyster sauce

10 ounces (283 g) dried rice vermicelli noodles or 21 ounces (600 g) fresh rice vermicelli noodles

7 ounces (200 g) leaf or iceberg lettuce, shredded or torn

3 ounces (90 g) herbs (such as mint, perilla, cilantro, and/or Asian basil leaves), chopped

8 rolls tofu wrapped in wild betel leaf (page 58) (optional)

2 tablespoons annatto oil (page 26), for drizzling

3 tablespoons crushed roasted peanuts, for garnish

SAUCE

2 cubes store-bought or homemade chao (page 22)

2 tablespoons fermented soybean sauce

½ cup (120 ml) water

2 tablespoons sugar

3 tablespoons vegetable oil

3 tablespoons thinly sliced leek (white part only)

1 tablespoon peanut butter

1. MAKE THE SALAD In a medium bowl, combine seitan, five-spice powder, lemongrass, 1 teaspoon of sugar, stock powder, pepper, 1 tablespoon of vegetable oil, soy sauce, and vegetarian oyster sauce. Mix well and let sit for 15 minutes.

2. Spread out the seitan slices on a sheet pan lined with parchment paper. Grill in the oven under the broiler or in an air fryer at 350°F (175°C) until slightly golden brown (10 to 15 minutes in the oven or 10 minutes in the air fryer).

3. MAKE THE SAUCE In a food processor, combine the chao cubes, fermented soybean sauce, water, and 2 tablespoons of sugar, and process until smooth. Set aside.

4. In a medium skillet, heat 3 tablespoons of vegetable oil over medium-low heat. When hot, add leek and cook and stir until golden brown (about 2 minutes). Using a slotted spoon, transfer to a small bowl.

5. Add the blended sauce and peanut butter to the remaining oil in the skillet and stir well. Bring to a boil, and then reduce the heat to low and simmer until slightly thickened (about 2 minutes).

6. If using dried vermicelli noodles, cook them following the instructions on the package.

7. Fill serving bowls about one-third with lettuce and herbs, and then layer about one-third of the cooked rice vermicelli noodles on top. Place a few pieces of grilled seitan and a couple rolls of tofu wrapped in wild betel leaf (if using). Drizzle the sauce and annatto oil over the top, sprinkle with roasted peanuts and fried leek, toss, and serve.

VERMICELLI NOODLE SALAD BOWL WITH FERMENTED SAUCE

Instead of the traditional pork and fermented anchovy sauce, this version (bún mắm nêm chay) uses chao and fermented soybean sauce to replicate the pungent flavor of mắm nêm.

SKILL LEVEL Moderate | **YIELD** 4 servings

SAUCE

3 cubes store-bought or homemade chao (page 22)

1 tablespoon chao brine

3 tablespoons fermented soybean sauce

½ cup (120 ml) water

½ cup (77 g) roughly chopped pineapple

3 tablespoons vegetable oil

1 leek (white part only), thinly sliced, plus 1 tablespoon, minced, divided

1 tablespoon minced lemongrass

2 tablespoons annatto oil (page 26)

1 tablespoon sugar, plus more to taste

1 teaspoon vegetable or mushroom stock powder

TOPPINGS AND NOODLES

½ cup (120 ml) vegetable oil

1 block (14 ounces/400 g) firm tofu, cut into 1-inch (2.5 cm) cubes

10½ ounces (300 g) fresh young jackfruit or breadfruit, peeled, or canned jackfruit, drained

10 ounces (283 g) dried rice vermicelli noodles or 21 ounces (600 g) fresh rice vermicelli noodles

10½ ounces (300 g) leaf or iceberg lettuce, shredded or torn

3½ ounces (100 g) fresh green herbs (such as mint, perilla, cilantro, and/or Asian basil leaves), chopped

2 tablespoons annatto oil (page 26)

½ cup (72 g) crushed roasted peanuts

1. MAKE THE SAUCE In a blender, combine the chao cubes, chao brine, fermented soybean sauce, and water and process until smooth. Add pineapple and process into a coarse purée.

2. In a small skillet, heat 3 tablespoons of vegetable oil over medium-low heat. When hot, add leek slices and cook and stir until golden (about 2 minutes). Leaving the oil in the skillet, use a slotted spoon to transfer fried leek to a small bowl and set aside.

3. Put skillet over medium-low heat, add minced leek, lemongrass, and 2 tablespoons of annatto oil, and cook and stir until fragrant (about 2 minutes). Add puréed mixture, sugar, and stock powder to pan, and simmer until bubbling (2 to 3 more minutes). Add more sugar if needed to get an equal balance of sweet and savory.

4. MAKE THE TOPPINGS AND NOODLES In a medium skillet, heat ½ cup (120 ml) of vegetable oil over medium-low heat. When hot, add tofu cubes and cook until golden brown on all sides (10 to 15 minutes). Transfer to a cooling rack or paper towel–lined plate to drain.

5. If using fresh young jackfruit, place it in a small saucepan and cover with water. Bring to a boil and cook until soft enough to be skewered with a fork or chopstick (20 to 25 minutes for fresh or 15 minutes for canned; if using breadfruit, boil for 10 to 15 minutes). Remove from heat, allow to cool, and then cut jackfruit into thin slices. Stack the slices on top of each other and cut along the grain into julienned strips (see Note on page 37).

6. If using dried vermicelli noodles, cook them following the instructions on the package.

7. Fill each serving bowl one-third with lettuce and herbs, and then add cooked vermicelli noodles on top. Place a few pieces of fried tofu and 2 tablespoons of jackfruit on top.

8. Drizzle the sauce and 2 tablespoons of annatto oil over the top, sprinkle with roasted peanuts and fried leek, toss, and serve.

SPICY NOODLE SOUP

This vegan version of bún bò Huế has a sweet broth comprised of various vegetables and fruits. Instead of beef, you'll use dried mock beef slices for the perfect balance of spicy, savory, and sweet.

SKILL LEVEL Advanced | **YIELD** 8 to 10 servings

1 medium chayote, peeled and cut into 1½-inch (4 cm) cubes

1 medium carrot, peeled and cut into 1½-inch (4 cm) cubes

1 medium corncob, cut into 1-inch (2.5 cm) thick rounds

1 small jicama, peeled and cut into 1½-inch (4 cm) cubes

1 medium apple or pear, peeled and cut into 1½-inch (4 cm) cubes

1 gallon (4 L) water

2 ounces (50 g) rock sugar

1 tablespoon salt

½ cup (120 ml) vegetable oil, divided

2 blocks (28 ounces/800 g) firm tofu

2 tablespoons minced lemongrass, plus 5 to 8 lemongrass stalks, trimmed and bruised (page 16)

1 tablespoon minced garlic

3 tablespoons minced leek (white part only)

1 tablespoon minced bird's eye chili pepper

2 tablespoons chili flakes or powder

1 tablespoon sugar

1 tablespoon vegetable or mushroom stock powder

2 ounces (56 g) dried mock beef slices, soaked (page 10)

10½ ounces (300 g) mushrooms (straw, shiitake, enoki, or beech), stems trimmed and cut into bite-size pieces

16 ounces (454 g) dried rice vermicelli noodles or 2¼ pounds (1 kg) fresh rice vermicelli noodles

2 ounces (56 g) cilantro, finely chopped, for garnish

3½ ounces (100 g) leaf or iceberg lettuce, shredded or torn, for serving

3 ounces (90 g) green herbs, (such as mint, perilla, cilantro, and/or Asian basil), chopped, for serving

3½ ounces (100 g) bean sprouts, for serving

3 ounces (90 g) banana blossom, prepped (page 15) and shredded, for serving

1 lime, cut into wedges, for serving

1. Place chayote, carrot, corn, jicama, and apple in a large stockpot, and then add the water, rock sugar, and salt. Bring to a boil, and then reduce the heat to medium-low and simmer, uncovered, until vegetables are sweet to the taste (about 1 hour).

2. Heat ¼ cup (60 ml) of the oil in a small skillet over medium-low heat. When hot, add the tofu and cook until golden brown on all sides (10 to 15 minutes). Transfer to a cooling rack or paper towel–lined plate to drain, and then cut into slices.

3. Heat the remaining ¼ cup (60 ml) oil in a medium skillet over low heat. When hot, add minced lemongrass, garlic, leek, chili pepper, bruised lemongrass stalks, chili flakes, sugar, and stock powder. Cook and stir until slightly golden (about 3 minutes). Remove from heat.

4. Using tongs or chopsticks, transfer lemongrass stalks to the large pot of vegetables. Reserve half of the cooked mixture in a small bowl to serve as a condiment with each bowl of soup.

5. Add the mock beef slices and mushrooms to the remaining half of mixture in the skillet and cook and stir over medium-low heat until tender (2 to 3 minutes). Add tofu slices, stir gently, and then remove from heat and set aside.

6. If using dried vermicelli, cook it following the package instructions. If using fresh, quickly blanch it in hot water if it has been refrigerated.

7. Fill one-third of each serving bowl with rice vermicelli noodles, and then top with mushrooms, tofu, and mock beef slices. Ladle hot broth over the top and garnish with chopped cilantro.

8. Serve with a platter of lettuce, herbs, bean sprouts, banana blossom, and lime wedges, along with the reserved condiment mixture.

STIR-FRIED NOODLES

This recipe (mì xào chay) calls for ramen noodles, which are usually vegan. On rare occasions, though, they're made with egg, so it's always wise for vegans to ask someone or check the ingredients label. You can also use udon, soba, glass, or rice noodles for this recipe.

SKILL LEVEL Moderate | **YIELD** 4 servings

SAUCE

1 tablespoon sugar

1 tablespoon soy sauce, plus
3 tablespoons for serving

1 tablespoon vegetarian oyster sauce

1 tablespoon ketchup

1 tablespoon sriracha

½ teaspoon vegetable or mushroom stock powder

¼ cup (60 ml) filtered water

STIR-FRY

¼ cup (60 ml) plus 3 tablespoons vegetable oil, divided

1 block (14 ounces/400 g) firm tofu

21 ounces (600 g) dried or 42 ounces (1.2 kg) fresh ramen noodles

1 tablespoon thinly sliced leek (white part only)

1 ounce (30 g) dried shiitake mushrooms, soaked (page 12) and sliced

3½ ounces (100 g) carrot, peeled and shredded

¾ ounce (20 g) garlic chives (or Chinese chives), cut into 2-inch (5 cm) lengths

3½ ounces (100 g) white or green cabbage, shredded

½ cup (50 g) roughly chopped Chinese celery (optional)

3½ ounces (100 g) mung bean sprouts

1 bird's eye chili pepper, sliced, for garnish

Soy sauce, for serving

1. MAKE THE SAUCE In a small bowl, whisk together sugar, soy sauce, vegetarian oyster sauce, ketchup, sriracha, stock powder, and filtered water until solids are dissolved. Set aside

2. MAKE THE STIR-FRY Heat ¼ cup (60 ml) of the vegetable oil in a small skillet over medium-low heat. When hot, add the tofu and cook until golden brown on all sides (10 to 15 minutes). Transfer to a cooling rack or paper towel–lined plate to drain. When cool, cut into ½-inch (1 cm) thick slices.

3. Fill a large saucepan halfway with water and bring to a boil over high heat. Blanch fresh ramen noodles until loosened (1 to 2 minutes). For dried ramen, follow the directions on the package, and then drain through a colander. Rinse several times with cold tap water to eliminate excess starch, and then drain well and set aside.

4. In a large skillet or wok, heat the remaining 3 tablespoons oil over medium-low heat. When hot, add leek and cook and stir until slightly golden brown (about 1 minute). Add mushrooms, tofu, carrot, and 2 tablespoons of the prepared sauce. Cook and stir until mushrooms are tender (about 2 minutes).

5. Add noodles to the skillet and stir well, adding more sauce gradually (1 to 2 tablespoons at a time), adjusting the amount to taste.

6. Add garlic chives, cabbage, celery (if using), and mung bean sprouts and stir well. Cook until wilted (1 to 2 more minutes).

7. Transfer to plates, garnish with chili pepper slices, and serve hot with a side of soy sauce.

RICE & STICKY RICE DISHES

As delicious as it is, if you think you are just going to find a recipe for a broken rice plate in this section, you are wrong! How about some fried rice in a pineapple or butternut squash? Or, maybe some sticky rice with mung beans and shallots? When you need to serve a side that goes beyond the basics, these variations on a familiar staple are sure to impress.

BROKEN RICE PLATE

Cơm tấm is an iconic dish from Southern Vietnam that features steamed broken rice topped with grilled pork chop, a piece of meatloaf, and shredded pork skin. This version calls for all the classic ingredients, except for the meats, of course. Broken rice (gạo tấm) is white jasmine rice that is fractured during the milling process and has a nutty taste.

SKILL LEVEL Advanced | **YIELD** 6 to 8 servings

BROKEN RICE

2¼ cups (520 ml) water

1 pound (454 g) broken rice (see Note on page 126), rinsed

VEGAN PORK CHOPS

1 tablespoon sesame oil

1 tablespoon vegetarian oyster sauce or soy sauce

1 tablespoon water

1 tablespoon sugar

2 tablespoons char siu seasoning mix

7 ounces (200 g) store-bought or homemade seitan (page 12), cut into ½-inch (1 cm) thick steaks, or 3½ ounces (100 g) textured vegetable protein (see Note on page 126), soaked for 15 minutes in warm water and excess water squeezed out

3 tablespoons vegetable oil

VEGAN SHREDDED PORK SKIN

½ cup (120 ml) plus 1 tablespoon vegetable oil, divided

1 ounce (28 g) glass noodles, divided

7 ounces (200 g) sweet potato, peeled and shredded, divided

7 ounces (200 g) taro (page 17), peeled and shredded, divided

1 block (14 ounces/400 g) firm tofu

1. MAKE THE BROKEN RICE Combine 2¼ cups (520 ml) of water and broken rice in a medium saucepan with a tight-fitting lid and stir. Bring to a boil, reduce heat to medium, and cook, uncovered, until the water level drops below the surface of the rice (about 5 minutes). Reduce heat to low, cover the pot, and simmer for an additional 15 minutes without lifting the lid. Remove from heat and let stand for an additional 5 minutes. Fluff rice with a chopstick or fork.

2. MAKE THE VEGAN PORK CHOPS In a large bowl, combine sesame oil, vegetarian oyster sauce, 1 tablespoon of water, 1 tablespoon of sugar, and char siu seasoning mix. Stir well until all solids are dissolved. Add seitan, toss to coat with the marinade, and let sit for 15 minutes.

3. In a medium skillet, heat 3 tablespoons of vegetable oil over medium-low heat. When hot, add the marinated seitan and cook until golden on both sides (about 2 minutes each side). Add the remaining marinade from the bowl and simmer on low for 2 minutes, or until thickened. Transfer to a plate and set aside.

4. MAKE THE VEGAN SHREDDED PORK SKIN Heat ½ cup of the vegetable oil in a small skillet over medium-low heat. When hot, add half of the glass noodles and cook until they puff up (about 5 seconds). Remove and place on a paper towel-lined plate to drain. Soak the remaining glass noodles in water for 10 minutes and drain.

5. Add half of the shredded sweet potato and half of the taro to the remaining hot oil in the pan and cook and stir until golden brown and crispy (3 to 5 minutes). Transfer to a paper towel-lined plate to drain.

6. Add the tofu block to the remaining hot oil in the pan and cook until golden brown on all sides (10 to 15 minutes). Transfer to a cooling rack or paper towel-lined plate to drain. When cool, cut tofu into 1-inch (2.5 cm) thick strips.

continued on page 126

continued from page 124

7 ounces (200 g) kohlrabi, peeled and shredded

½ teaspoon salt

½ teaspoon vegetable or mushroom stock powder

2 ounces (56 g) sticky rice, rinsed and drained

VEGAN MEATLOAF

1 block (14 ounces/400 g) firm tofu, finely crushed with a fork

2 ounces (56 g) carrot, peeled and finely shredded

1 ounce (28 g) glass noodles, soaked until soft and drained

1 ounce (28 g) dried wood ear mushrooms, soaked (page 13) and finely shredded

1 teaspoon vegetable or mushroom stock powder

½ teaspoon sugar

1 tablespoon minced leek (white part only)

1 tablespoon cornstarch

2 tablespoons water

2 teaspoons annatto oil (page 26)

FOR SERVING

1 recipe scallion oil (page 26)

1 medium cucumber, sliced

1 medium plum tomato, sliced

1 cup (240 ml) vegan fish dipping sauce (page 20)

7. In a large skillet, heat the remaining 1 tablespoon vegetable oil over medium-low heat. Add the kohlrabi, remaining sweet potato and taro, salt, and ½ teaspoon of stock powder, and cook until soft (about 5 minutes). Add fried tofu strips and soaked glass noodles, cook and stir for 1 more minute, and then remove from heat to cool.

8. In a small, clean skillet, toast sticky rice over medium heat until golden brown (about 5 minutes), stirring constantly. Use a spice grinder, mortar and pestle, or food processor to grind the toasted rice into a powder.

9. In a large bowl, combine the deep-fried glass noodles, sweet potato, taro, tofu mixture, and toasted rice powder, and toss well.

10. MAKE THE VEGAN MEATLOAF In a separate large bowl, combine the crushed tofu, shredded carrot, soaked glass noodles, wood ear mushrooms, 1 teaspoon of stock powder, ½ teaspoon of sugar, and minced leek. Mix and let sit for 15 minutes. Transfer to an 8½ by 4½-inch (21 by 11 cm) or a 6-inch (15 cm) square heat-proof or oven-safe container.

11. Fill a steamer halfway with water and place the vegan meatloaf in the basket. Wrap the steamer lid in a large kitchen towel and tie the corners over the handle. This will absorb excess steam and prevent it from dropping back down in the meatloaf. Bring the water to a boil, cover, and steam until set (about 20 minutes). Alternatively, you can bake the vegan meatloaf in a preheated oven at 375°F (180°C) until it forms into a cake (about 20 minutes).

12. In a small bowl, mix cornstarch, 2 tablespoons of water, and annatto oil, and stir to dissolve starch. With a basting or pastry brush, brush mixture on surface of vegan meatloaf, and then steam or bake for 5 more minutes. Let completely cool, and then cut into 1-inch (2.5 cm) thick slices.

13. FOR SERVING To shape the broken rice into a small dome, fill a small rice bowl with cooked broken rice and press it gently into the bowl. Invert the rice onto a serving plate and top with 1 teaspoon of scallion oil. Place a slice of vegan meatloaf and vegan pork chop on the side, along with a scoop of vegan shredded pork skin, and serve with cucumber and tomato slices, and a bowl of vegan fish dipping sauce.

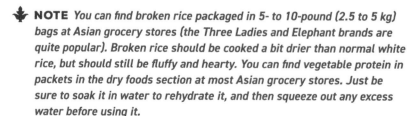 **NOTE** *You can find broken rice packaged in 5- to 10-pound (2.5 to 5 kg) bags at Asian grocery stores (the Three Ladies and Elephant brands are quite popular). Broken rice should be cooked a bit drier than normal white rice, but should still be fluffy and hearty. You can find vegetable protein in packets in the dry foods section at most Asian grocery stores. Just be sure to soak it in water to rehydrate it, and then squeeze out any excess water before using it.*

STICKY RICE COATED WITH MUNG BEANS

What makes xôi vò different from other kinds of steamed sticky rice is that its grains are coated with mung bean powder and separated from one another in the final dish. The version of this dish made in Northern Vietnam only requires a handful of ingredients.

SKILL LEVEL Moderate | **YIELD** 4 servings

2 tablespoons vegetable oil

2 ounces (56 g) shallots, thinly sliced

1 cup (200 g) sticky rice, rinsed, soaked for 4 to 8 hours, and drained

½ recipe mashed mung beans (page 11), divided

⅔ teaspoon salt, divided

3 tablespoons full-fat, unsweetened coconut milk (optional)

1 tablespoon sugar (optional)

1. Heat oil in a small pan over medium-low heat. Add shallots and cook and stir until golden brown (about 2 minutes). Using a slotted spoon, the fried shallots to a small bowl and set aside. Reserve the shallot oil in the pan.

2. In a large bowl, combine soaked rice, half of the mashed mung beans, and ⅓ teaspoon of the salt, and toss well.

3. Fill a large pot that can hold an 8- to-10-inch (20 to 25 cm) steamer basket with water until it is at least 1 inch (2.5 cm) below the base of the basket, and bring to a boil over medium-high heat. Line steamer basket with a piece of banana leaf or parchment paper to prevent rice from falling through the grates. Spread the rice–mung bean mixture in an even layer in the steamer basket, and then poke a few holes through the layer. Wrap the steamer lid in a large kitchen towel and tie the corners over the handle to absorb excess steam. Cover the steamer basket, place it on top of the boiling pot, and steam for 15 minutes.

4. In a small bowl, combine unsweetened coconut milk (if using), sugar (if using), and remaining ⅓ teaspoon salt. Stir until solids are dissolved, and then drizzle over the rice. Fluff rice with chopsticks or a fork, and then steam for 5 more minutes.

5. Transfer rice to a large bowl and combine with the fried shallots and 1 tablespoon of the reserved shallot oil. Toss well, add the rest of the mashed mung beans, and then toss again. If you see any lumps, gently rub them with your hands until the rice grains are separated and well coated with the mashed mung beans.

6. Serve at room temperature.

PINEAPPLE FRIED RICE

This dish from Thailand (cơm chiên trái thơm) has become one of the most popular ways to prepare fried rice in Vietnam. The refreshing, sweet-and-sour pineapple balances out the fried rice in an exquisite way, and the roasted cashew nuts add a special crunch. It is colorful, delicious, and beautifully served in a pineapple.

SKILL LEVEL Moderate | **YIELD** 2 servings

1 whole, medium-ripe pineapple (about 3 pounds/1.5 kg)

3½ ounces (100 g) firm tofu, cut into 1-inch (2.5 cm) cubes

¼ teaspoon five-spice or curry powder

½ teaspoon salt, divided

¼ teaspoon freshly ground black pepper

3 tablespoons vegetable oil

¼ cup (40 g) diced yellow onion

¼ cup (30 g) diced carrot

¼ cup (40 g) green peas

1 cup (140 g) leftover cooked long-grain white rice (see Note)

¼ teaspoon turmeric powder (optional)

½ teaspoon vegetable or mushroom stock powder

2 tablespoons soy sauce or vegan fish sauce (page 20)

1 ounce (28 g) scallion, finely chopped

10 roasted cashew nuts

1. Cut the pineapple in half lengthwise through the green top, and then run a sharp paring knife around the inside of both halves, closer to the peel, to create a bowl shape. Score the pineapple flesh into a grid, making each piece around ½ inch (1 cm) wide. Use a spoon to scoop out the flesh, remove and discard the core, and then dice the flesh.

2. In a small bowl, toss the tofu with the five-spice powder, ¼ teaspoon of the salt, and pepper. In a medium skillet, heat oil over medium-high heat. When hot, add the tofu and cook until golden brown on all sides (about 4 minutes). Remove tofu and transfer to a paper towel–lined plate to drain.

3. Add the onion to the remaining oil in the skillet and cook and stir over medium heat until translucent (about 2 minutes). Add carrot and green peas, and cook and stir until tender (8 to 10 minutes).

4. Add the diced pineapple, fried tofu, leftover rice, and turmeric powder (if using) to make it yellow, and toss well. Cook until rice is yellow (about 2 minutes), and then season with remaining ¼ teaspoon salt, stock powder, and soy sauce. Use a spatula to break up any rice lumps and cook and stir for about 3 more minutes. Stir in scallion and turn off heat.

5. Divide the pineapple fried rice between the hollowed-out pineapple halves. Sprinkle cashews on top and serve hot.

🍂 **NOTE** *It is best to use leftover long-grain white rice for fried rice as it's already cooked and has a dry texture, making it ideal for stir-frying and preventing clumping. Additionally, using leftover rice is a great way to reduce food waste.*

STICKY RICE WITH MUNG BEANS AND FRIED SHALLOTS

Xôi xéo is a classic Northern Vietnam take on mung bean sticky rice. It is a typical breakfast that many Hanoians love. This dish features soft, chewy, golden sticky rice that gets its color from turmeric. The wholesome mung beans coupled with crispy, fried shallots are pure melt-in-your-mouth goodness!

SKILL LEVEL Advanced | **YIELD** 6 servings

STICKY RICE

2 cups (400 g) sticky rice, rinsed, soaked for 4 to 8 hours, and drained

¼ teaspoon salt

¼ teaspoon turmeric powder

3 pandan leaves (optional)

TOPPINGS

¼ cup (60 ml) vegetable oil

2 shallots or 1 medium yellow onion

1½ teaspoons sugar, divided

½ cup (100 g) peeled split mung beans, rinsed, soaked, and drained (page 11)

¼ teaspoon salt

1. MAKE THE STICKY RICE In a medium bowl, toss the soaked sticky rice with salt and turmeric powder.

2. Fill a large pot that can hold an 8- to 10-inch (20 to 25 cm) steamer basket with water until it is at least 1 inch (2.5 cm) below the base of the basket, and bring to a boil over medium-high heat. Use a piece of banana leaf or parchment paper to prevent rice from falling through the grates and sticking. Spread the sticky rice in an even layer in the steamer basket, and then poke a few holes through the layer. Tie pandan leaves into knots (if using) and place on the rice. Wrap the steamer lid in a large kitchen towel and tie the corners of the fabric over the handle. This will absorb excess steam and prevent it from dropping back down in the rice. Cover the steamer basket and place it on top of the boiling pot. Steam until the rice is no longer opaque and is tender, sticky, and slightly chewy (35 to 40 minutes).

3. MAKE THE TOPPINGS In a small skillet, heat oil over medium-low heat. When hot, add shallots and cook and stir until golden brown (about 2 minutes). Using a slotted spoon, transfer to a paper towel–lined plate to drain. Stir in 1 teaspoon of the sugar to help shallots remain crisp. Transfer remaining shallot oil to a small bowl and set aside.

4. Cook mung bean until tender following the instructions on page 11, but do not mash them. Place cooked beans, 1 teaspoon of reserved shallot oil, remaining ½ teaspoon sugar, and salt in a food processor and blend into a smooth paste. Transfer to the center of a large piece of plastic wrap. Gather the edges of the wrap and twist and shape the mixture into a large ball. Remove the plastic wrap and place the ball in a medium bowl.

5. Fluff the cooked sticky rice with chopsticks and divide among serving plates. Use a knife to shave the mung bean ball into thin slices and place the slices over the rice.

6. Top with fried shallots, drizzle with remaining shallot oil, and serve.

BLACK BEAN STICKY RICE

Black bean sticky rice (xôi đậu đen) is popular in every region of Vietnam. Street vendors used to wrap each serving of sticky rice in a large piece of banana leaf to keep it hot and smelling delicious. Topped with shredded coconut, roasted peanuts, and sesame seeds, this dish makes a yummy and filling breakfast for kids, which is why so many natives have fond childhood memories of it.

SKILL LEVEL Moderate | **YIELD** 4 servings

BLACK BEANS

1 cup (180 g) dried black beans, rinsed, soaked for 8 hours, and drained

3 cups (720 ml) water

STICKY RICE

1 cup (200 g) sticky rice, rinsed

½ teaspoon salt

1 teaspoon vegetable oil

3 pandan leaves (optional)

TOPPINGS

3 tablespoons crushed roasted peanuts

1 tablespoon toasted sesame seeds

2 teaspoons sugar

½ teaspoon salt

2 ounces (56 g) shredded coconut

1. MAKE THE BLACK BEANS In a medium saucepan, combine soaked black beans and water and bring to a boil over high heat. Simmer over low heat until beans are soft but still holding their shape (about 45 minutes). (To save time, you can also cook the beans in a pressure cooker for 25 minutes). Drain beans, reserving the cooking water in a bowl.

2. MAKE THE STICKY RICE Soak the rinsed sticky rice in the reserved bean cooking water for 4 to 8 hours. Drain rice in a colander and shake off excess water.

3. In a medium bowl, toss soaked sticky rice with the drained cooked beans, salt, and vegetable oil.

4. Fill a large pot that can hold an 8- to 10-inch (20 to 25.5 cm) steamer basket with water until it is just 1 inch (2.5 cm) below the base of the basket, and bring to a boil over medium-high heat. Line steamer basket with a piece of banana leaf or parchment paper to prevent rice from falling through the grates and sticking. Spread sticky rice–beans mixture in an even layer in the steamer basket, and then poke a few holes through the layer. Tie pandan leaves into knots (if using), place on rice, and then wrap the steamer lid in a large kitchen towel and tie the corners of the fabric over the handle. This will absorb excess steam and prevent it from dropping back down in the rice. Cover the steamer basket, place on top of the boiling pot, and steam until rice becomes tender, sticky, and slightly chewy (35 to 40 minutes).

5. MAKE THE TOPPINGS In a small bowl, combine peanuts, sesame seeds, sugar, and salt and mix well.

6. Fluff cooked sticky rice and black beans with chopsticks and divide among serving plates. Top with peanut–sesame seed mixture and shredded coconut. Serve hot.

BROWN RICE IN BUTTERNUT SQUASH

If you're looking for a nutritious weekend meal for the family, give this brown rice in butternut squash (cơm gạo lứt bí đỏ) a try. In addition to the star ingredients, you'll add a medley of carrots, tofu, and raisins. It's as pretty and healthy as it is yummy.

SKILL LEVEL Moderate | **YIELD** 2 servings

2 pear-shaped butternut or kabocha squash or sugar pumpkins (about 2 pounds/1 kg)

1 cup (200 g) long- or short-grain brown rice, rinsed and drained

1½ cups (360 ml) water

3 tablespoons vegetable oil

2 ounces (56 g) firm tofu, cut into ½-inch (1 cm) cubes

1 tablespoon minced leek (white part only)

2 ounces (56 g) fresh straw or shiitake mushrooms, stems removed and diced

1 ounce (28 g) green peas

2 ounces (56 g) fresh or frozen lotus root (see Note), diced

2 ounces (56 g) carrot, diced

½ cup (73 g) raisins

2 teaspoons soy sauce or vegan fish sauce (page 20)

½ teaspoon vegetable or mushroom stock powder

½ teaspoon sesame oil

1. Cut off the upper dense part of the butternut squash and save it to make pumpkin and peanut soup (page 88). Scoop out the seeds to create a bowl. For a nicer presentation, you can carve the rim of the squash bowl with a serrated knife, using a zigzag motion.

2. In a medium saucepan, combine the rice and water, and bring to a boil over medium-high heat. Reduce heat to low, cover, and simmer until crater-like steam holes appear in the surface of the rice (about 35 minutes). Turn off the heat and let rice sit, covered, for another 10 minutes. Fluff well with chopsticks or a fork. (You can also cook the rice in a rice cooker, if you prefer).

3. In a large skillet, heat vegetable oil over medium-low heat. When hot, add tofu and cook until golden brown on all sides (about 5 minutes). Use a slotted spoon to transfer to a plate.

4. Add leek to the remaining oil in the skillet and cook and stir until slightly golden (about 1 minute). Return tofu to skillet and add mushrooms, peas, lotus root, carrot, and raisins, and cook and stir until the vegetables have softened (4 to 5 minutes).

5. Add cooked rice, soy sauce, and stock powder, and mix well. Remove pan from heat.

6. Spoon the filling into the two squash halves, and then drizzle sesame oil over the filling.

7. Fill a steamer halfway with water and place the squash halves in the basket. Bring the water to a boil, cover, and steam until you can pierce the squash with the tip of a knife (20 to 30 minutes, depending on the thickness of the flesh). When done, use steamer tongs or oven mitts to carefully transfer to plates and serve hot.

 NOTE *Fresh lotus root is usually sold in two- or three-link segments in the produce section at Asian grocery stores. You might also be able to find slices frozen or canned.*

BREADS & DUMPLINGS

Many people think making dough is an overly complicated process, but this is a misconception. Armed with a few tips and tricks, not only will you be prepping and kneading your own dough in no time, but you will also be filling it with an array of delicious, satisfying ingredients! From the simple prep of bánh mì to instructions on folding rice pyramid dumplings, you will soon be impressing everyone with your homemade Vietnamese dumplings and crêpes.

BÁNH MÌ

During the French colonization in the mid-nineteenth century, people started putting local Vietnamese ingredients on French baguettes and sold them as affordable sandwiches. Bánh mì has remained a popular street food ever since. It's also consistently ranked as one of the best sandwiches in the world. The basic components include pâté, a main protein (such as egg, cold cuts, grilled meat, or tofu), pickles, fresh herbs, and sauce. However, the fillings are versatile and vary by region. The main proteins for this vegan bánh mì are tofu and seitan flavored with char siu, which is a seasoning mix to make Chinese barbecue pork.

SKILL LEVEL Advanced | **YIELD** 8 servings

VEGAN PÂTÉ

3½ ounces (100 g) dried white beans, soaked in 2 cups (480 ml) water for at least 8 hours (or 10½ ounces/300 g canned white beans, drained, for a quicker version)

1 tablespoon vegetable oil

1 tablespoon minced leek (white part only)

1 tablespoon minced lemongrass

1 Japanese eggplant, cut into ½-inch (1 cm) thick slices

10 raw cashew nuts, soaked in warm water for 30 minutes and peeled

1 tablespoon sugar

2 tablespoons soy sauce

½ teaspoon salt

½ teaspoon unsweetened cocoa powder

Freshly ground black pepper, to taste

¼ cup (60 ml) vegan butter or margarine, melted

continued on following page

1. MAKE THE VEGAN PÂTÉ If using canned beans, skip to step 2. Place dried beans in a medium saucepan and fill with enough water to cover. Bring to a boil over high heat, and then cover and simmer on low heat until beans are tender but not mushy (20 to 30 minutes). Remove from heat and drain.

2. In a medium skillet, heat 1 tablespoon of oil over medium-low heat. When hot, add leek and lemongrass, and cook and stir until fragrant (about 2 minutes). Add Japanese eggplant and cashews, and cook and stir until slightly browned and softened (3 to 5 minutes). Add precooked or canned white beans, sugar, soy sauce, and salt. Cook and stir for 2 minutes, and then turn off heat and let cool.

3. Transfer cooled mixture to a blender or food processor, add cocoa powder, and process until smooth.

4. Pour the purée into a 2-cup (480 ml) container, sprinkle with ground pepper, and drizzle melted margarine on top. Cover and refrigerate for 4 hours.

5. MAKE THE FILLING In a large bowl, combine lemongrass, leek, char siu seasoning mix, vegetarian oyster sauce, water, sugar, salt, and ¼ teaspoon of ground pepper, and stir well. Cut tofu into 1-inch (2.5 cm) thick steaks and add to bowl along with seitan. Toss well to coat with sauce, and let marinate for 30 minutes.

6. Scrape off the minced aromatics and shake off excess marinade from the tofu and seitan, but leave remaining marinade in the bowl.

continued from previous page

FILLING

1 tablespoon minced lemongrass

1 tablespoon minced leek
(white part only)

2 tablespoons char siu
seasoning mix

1 tablespoon vegetarian
oyster sauce

3 tablespoons water

1 tablespoon sugar

½ teaspoon salt

¼ teaspoon freshly ground
black pepper

1 block (14 ounces/400 g) firm tofu

3½ ounces (100 g) store-bought
or homemade seitan (page 12)

¼ cup (60 ml) vegetable oil

SANDWICHES

8 Vietnamese baguette loaves
or 8 sections (7 inches/18 cm long)
French baguette(s)

½ recipe pickled carrots
and daikon (page 33)

2 ounces (56 g) cilantro,
roughly chopped

1 medium cucumber, peeled,
seeds removed, and cut lengthwise
into 3-inch (7.5 cm) slices

3 jalapeño peppers, sliced on
the bias (optional)

7. In a medium skillet, heat ¼ cup (60 ml) of oil over medium heat. When hot, add tofu and seitan, and cook until golden brown on all sides (about 10 minutes). Remove from heat, let cool, and cut both into slices.

8. Put reserved marinade in a small saucepan and simmer over low heat until slightly thickened (2 to 3 minutes). Strain through a fine-mesh sieve into a small bowl and set aside.

9. ASSEMBLE Cut open each baguette lengthwise. Spread a thin layer of pâté on one side, and then drizzle with sauce. Add pickled carrots and daikon, cilantro, cucumber, tofu, seitan, and jalapeño pepper slices (if using), and serve immediately.

NOTE *If you want to prepare this recipe in stages, you can store the vegan pâté in the refrigerator for up to 1 week and the pickled carrots and daikon for up to 2 weeks.*

RICE PYRAMID DUMPLINGS

Bánh giò is a common breakfast in Northern Vietnam. This is a good example of how Vietnamese people turn basic and simple ingredients into masterpieces. In this recipe, you'll learn how to make a vegan version of bánh giò that still retains the traditional flavor.

SKILL LEVEL Advanced | **YIELD** 14 dumplings

FILLING

1 tablespoon vegetable oil

1 tablespoon minced leek (white part only)

2 ounces (56 g) dried wood ear mushrooms, soaked (page 13) and minced

2 ounces (56 g) dried shiitake mushrooms, soaked (page 12) and minced

2 ounces (56 g) king oyster mushrooms, stems trimmed and minced

½ teaspoon salt

1 teaspoon sugar

1 teaspoon soy sauce or vegan fish sauce (page 20)

1 teaspoon vegetable or mushroom stock powder, to taste

½ teaspoon freshly ground black pepper

WRAPPERS AND BATTER

14 squares (10 by 10 inches/ 25 by 25 cm) banana leaves, prepped (page 15)

14 squares (10 by 10 inches/ 25 by 25 cm) plastic wrap

continued on following page

1. MAKE THE FILLING Heat 1 tablespoon of oil in a medium skillet over medium-low heat. When hot, add leek and cook and stir until fragrant (about 1 minute). Add minced mushrooms, ½ teaspoon of salt, sugar, soy sauce, and stock powder. Cook and stir over medium heat until the mushrooms are tender (about 2 minutes), and then remove from heat and stir in pepper.

2. PREPARE THE WRAPPERS Stack the banana leaves on top of each other, with the darker, shiny side of each leaf facedown, inserting a square of plastic wrap under each leaf for support. Lift up one corner of a leaf square and fold diagonally toward the opposite corner. Then, fold again in half to form a smaller triangle. Repeat with remaining leaves and plastic wrap.

3. MAKE THE BATTER (SEE NOTE ON PAGE 142) In a large saucepan, combine rice flour and tapioca starch. Slowly whisk in broth to prevent lumps from forming. When mixture is smooth, whisk in 2 tablespoons of oil and 1 teaspoon of salt. Cook the batter over high heat, whisking constantly, until a viscous paste begins to form on the bottom of the pan (about 5 minutes). Immediately reduce heat to low and whisk vigorously until batter thickens to the consistency of mashed potatoes (5 to 8 minutes). It is okay if it is still a bit lumpy at this point. During the last few minutes of cooking, you may need to switch to a wooden spoon or a rubber spatula as the paste becomes too heavy to whisk. Remove from heat and continue stirring until completely smooth (about 1 minute).

continued from previous page

1 cup (155 g) rice flour

2 cups (260 g) tapioca starch
or cornstarch

6 cups (1.4 L) unsalted vegetable
broth or fresh unsweetened
coconut water

2 tablespoons vegetable oil,
plus more for greasing wrappers
and batter

1 teaspoon salt

FOR SERVING

½ cup (120 ml) vegan fish
dipping sauce (page 20)

¼ cup (60 ml) sriracha sauce
(optional)

4. Open a wrapper triangle and hold the point securely in one hand, keeping the sealed part next to your thumb. The opening should form a pocket to keep everything inside. Lightly oil the opening to prevent sticking. Dip a metal spoon in oil, and then scoop a heaping tablespoon of the paste into the opening. Use the back of the spoon to spread out and push it into the point. Scoop 2 tablespoons of the mushroom filling onto the dough, and then scoop 1 to 2 tablespoons of the batter on top. Spread it around to cover all the mince.

5. First, fold up the bottom corner of the wrapper, being held by your thumb, to cover the paste, and then tightly fold in each side. Finally, fold over the top corner, tucking its point into the base of the wrap. You should now have a nice pyramid with a flat base. Repeat to assemble the remaining dumplings.

6. Fill a steamer halfway with water and arrange the dumplings in the basket. Bring the water to a boil, cover, and steam on medium-high until the paste becomes translucent (about 20 minutes). Use tongs to remove the dumplings and allow to cool. Freshly steamed dumplings collapse easily when unwrapped, so let cool completely or chill in the refrigerator overnight, and then reheat them before serving. You can store the dumplings with the wrapper on for up to 1 week in the refrigerator.

7. FOR SERVING Microwave the dumplings on high for 1 minute. Open the seal to remove the wrappers and serve on a plate with vegan fish dipping sauce and sriracha (if using).

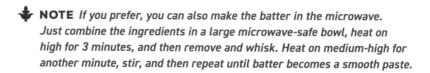 **NOTE** *If you prefer, you can also make the batter in the microwave. Just combine the ingredients in a large microwave-safe bowl, heat on high for 3 minutes, and then remove and whisk. Heat on medium-high for another minute, stir, and then repeat until batter becomes a smooth paste.*

STEAMED BUNS

No doubt, the original idea for bánh bao came from Chinese steamed buns (baozi).
However, this perfect on-the-go breakfast has been adapted with Vietnamese flavors and
become a staple. In this version, you use char siu seasoning mix (or turmeric powder,
if you prefer) to re-create the flavor of the original Chinese barbecue pork buns.

SKILL LEVEL Advanced | **YIELD** 8 large buns

DOUGH

1 cup (240 ml) lukewarm
(104°F/40°C) almond or soy milk

2 teaspoons instant dry yeast

½ teaspoon salt

½ cup (100 g) plus 1 tablespoon
sugar, divided

3½ cups (500 g) all-purpose flour,
plus more for dusting

2 teaspoons baking powder

2 tablespoons vegetable oil

FILLING

1 block (14 ounces/400 g) firm tofu,
mashed

1 ounce (28 g) dried shiitake
mushrooms, soaked (page 12)
and minced

1 ounce (28 g) dried wood ear
mushrooms, soaked (page 13)
and minced

1 tablespoon minced leek
(white part only)

½ cup (65 g) peeled and diced carrot
or water chestnuts

2 ounces (56 g) vermicelli or glass
noodles, finely chopped

2 tablespoons tapioca starch

1 tablespoon vegetarian oyster sauce

1 teaspoon sesame oil

¼ teaspoon freshly ground
black pepper

2 tablespoons char siu seasoning mix
or ½ teaspoon turmeric powder

1. MAKE THE DOUGH In a small bowl, combine lukewarm almond milk, yeast, salt, and 1 tablespoon of the sugar. Stir until yeast and sugar are completely dissolved, and then let sit for 5 minutes.

2. In a large bowl, combine flour, remaining ½ cup sugar, and baking powder. Make a hole in the center, add yeast mixture and vegetable oil, and then stir with a wooden spoon until well combined.

3. Turn out mixture on a floured work surface and knead until a smooth dough forms (10 to 15 minutes). Place dough back in bowl, cover with a damp kitchen towel, and let rest in a warm place (about 99°F/37°C) until it doubles in size (about 1 hour).

4. MAKE THE FILLING In a separate large bowl, combine mashed tofu, mushrooms, leek, carrot, noodles, tapioca starch, vegetarian oyster sauce, sesame oil, pepper, and char siu seasoning mix. Cover and leave to marinate for 30 minutes, and then divide into 8 equal-size portions.

5. Lightly dust work surface with flour, transfer dough, and knead again to remove air bubbles (about 2 minutes). Divide into 8 equal-size portions and shape each into a smooth ball. Cover dough balls with a kitchen towel and let rest for 10 minutes.

6. Flatten each dough ball into a round disc, about ½ inch (1 cm) thick. Pinch the edges so they are thinner than the centers, and then spoon filling into the center of each. Gather the edges and pinch to seal. As you finish each bun, slip it back under the damp kitchen towel and leave to rest for 15 minutes.

7. Fill a steamer halfway with water, and then place the buns in the steamer basket, leaving a generous amount of space between them so they have room to rise. Bring the water to a boil and then wrap the steamer lid in a towel and tie the corners of the fabric over the handle. This will absorb the excess steam. Steam until buns are dry and fluffy (20 to 25 minutes). Serve warm.

8. The buns will keep in the refrigerator for up to 1 week or the freezer for up to 3 months. To reheat buns, just steam them for 5 minutes or put them in the microwave on high for 2 minutes.

STEAMED RICE CAKES

Bánh bèo is a popular street food that originated in the imperial city of Huế. You will need molds to make it—any round ceramic condiment bowls 2 to 3 inches (5 to 7.5 cm) in diameter and 1 inch (2.5 cm) high will work. Ramekins or silicone muffin cups also work, but pour a thinner layer of batter (½ inch/1 cm thick) for each cake.

SKILL LEVEL Advanced | **YIELD** 8 to 10 servings (about 50 rice cakes)

STEAMED RICE CAKES

3 cups (400 g) rice flour

¾ cup (100 g) tapioca starch

1½ teaspoons salt, divided

4 cups (1 L) water

1 tablespoon vegetable oil

TOPPING

3½ ounces (100 g) fresh shiitake mushrooms, stems trimmed and roughly chopped

3½ ounces (100 g) fresh mushrooms (straw, button, king oyster, or similar), stems trimmed and roughly chopped

3½ ounces (100 g) carrot, peeled and roughly chopped

3 tablespoons vegetable oil, divided

1 tablespoon chopped leek (white part only)

1 teaspoon salt, divided

½ teaspoon mushroom or vegetable stock powder

½ cup (120 ml) water

½ cup (100 g) peeled split mung beans, rinsed, soaked, and drained (page 11)

¼ cup (60 ml) full-fat, unsweetened coconut milk

2 teaspoons sugar

FOR SERVING

½ cup (72 g) crushed roasted peanuts

1 cup (40 g) croutons (optional)

½ cup (120 ml) vegan fish dipping sauce (page 20)

1. MAKE THE STEAMED RICE CAKES In a large bowl, combine rice flour, tapioca starch, ½ teaspoon of salt, and 4 cups (1 L) of water. Whisk until well combined and set aside for 1 hour. Whisk in 1 teaspoon of salt and 1 tablespoon of oil.

2. Fill a steamer halfway with water and arrange molds in the basket. Bring the water to a boil, cover, and steam until molds are hot (about 2 minutes). Uncover and pour batter about ⅔ inch (1.7 cm) deep into each mold. Wrap the steamer lid with a large kitchen towel by tying the corners of the fabric over the handle. This will absorb some of the excess steam. Steam the cakes until they are firm and a shallow hollow has formed in the centers (3 to 5 minutes). Remove molds with tongs and set aside to cool. Continue steaming in batches, stirring batter each time before adding to the molds.

3. MAKE THE TOPPING Place mushrooms in a blender or food processor, pulse until they are finely chopped, and then transfer to a small bowl. Repeat with the carrot.

4. In a small skillet, heat 2 tablespoons of the oil over medium-low heat. Add the leek and cook and stir until fragrant (about 1 minute). Reserve 1 tablespoon of fried leek oil in a small bowl, then add mushrooms, ¼ teaspoon of the salt, and stock powder to the skillet. Cook and stir until mushrooms are fully cooked (3 to 5 minutes). Transfer to a bowl to cool.

5. Add the remaining 1 tablespoon oil to the same skillet, along with the carrot and ¼ teaspoon of the salt. Cook and stir until soft (about 2 minutes), and then transfer to a separate bowl to cool.

6. Combine ½ cup (120 ml) of water and mung beans in a small saucepan and stir. Bring water to a boil, and then cook over medium heat, uncovered, until water is mostly evaporated (about 5 minutes). Add coconut milk, sugar, and the remaining ½ teaspoon salt. Bring to a boil again and cook on low heat until all liquid is gone (3 to 5 more minutes). Transfer to a food processor and pulse until puréed.

7. FOR SERVING Run the tip of a serving knife or spoon handle around the edges of the rice cakes to loosen and remove from the molds. Arrange them on a platter and drizzle with reserved fried leek oil. Spread some mung bean paste on top of each rice cake, followed by the carrot, mushrooms, roasted peanuts, and croutons (if using). Drizzle vegan fish dipping sauce on top and serve immediately.

STEAMED RICE ROLLS

Originally from Northern Vietnam, bánh cuốn (which translates to "rolled cake") are thin, steamed rice flour rolls. The rice crêpes used are similar to delicate rice noodle sheets, but smaller, thinner, and more translucent. This is a time-consuming recipe, and, unfortunately, the specialized steamer necessary to make bánh cuốn is hard to find outside of Vietnam; however, you can use an 8-inch (20 cm) lightweight nonstick pan instead.

SKILL LEVEL Advanced | **YIELD** 5 or 6 rolls

FILLING

¼ cup (60 ml) vegetable oil

1 tablespoon chopped leek (white part only)

2 ounces (50 g) dried wood ear mushrooms, soaked (page 13) and julienned (see Note on page 37)

1 medium carrot, peeled and julienned (see Note on page 37)

3½ ounces (100 g) jicama, peeled and julienned (see Note on page 37)

2 ounces (56 g) fried tofu (page 11), cut into strips

½ teaspoon salt

1 teaspoon vegetable or mushroom stock powder

1 teaspoon soy sauce or vegan fish sauce (page 20)

CRÊPES

7 ounces (200 g) rice flour

7 ounces (200 g) tapioca starch

4 cups (1 L) water

1 tablespoon vegetable oil, plus more for greasing pan

1 teaspoon salt

FOR SERVING

1 medium cucumber, julienned (see Note on page 37)

7 ounces (200 g) mung bean sprouts, blanched

1 cup (240 ml) vegan fish dipping sauce (page 20)

1. MAKE THE FILLING Heat ¼ cup (60 ml) of vegetable oil in a medium skillet over medium-low heat. When hot, add leek and cook and stir until golden brown (1 to 2 minutes). Transfer to a small bowl along with most of the oil (leave about 1 tablespoon of leek and oil in the skillet).

2. Return pan to heat and add mushrooms, carrot, jicama, fried tofu, salt, stock powder, and soy sauce. Cook and stir over high heat until vegetables have softened but still retain some crispness (about 3 minutes), and then transfer to a medium bowl to cool.

3. MAKE THE CRÊPES In a large bowl, combine rice flour, tapioca starch, water, 1 tablespoon of vegetable oil, and salt, and stir well until flour is dissolved. Let the batter rest for at least 1 hour or overnight.

4. Grease a large plate, tray, or cutting board with some of the remaining leek oil and grease an 8-inch (20 cm) nonstick pan with a very thin layer of vegetable oil.

5. Heat the nonstick pan over medium heat. When it's hot, stir the batter and pour about ¼ cup (60 ml) of it into the pan. While wearing oven mitts, tilt the pan in a circular motion to thoroughly coat the bottom with batter and create an evenly round crêpe. Cover and allow the crêpe to steam until it turns translucent (about 1 minute). Uncover, lift the pan, and flip the crêpe out onto your pre-greased plate, tray, or cutting board. (Use a spatula to loosen before flipping if some parts are sticking to the pan). Repeat with remaining batter.

6. While waiting for the next crêpe to steam, top the finished one with 2 tablespoons of the filling. Spread it across the crêpe until it is closer to the bottom end, and then lift up the bottom end and roll it over the filling. Secure the roll closed, gently but tightly.

7. FOR SERVING Arrange the rolls on a platter and spoon the reserved fried leek and oil on top. Serve with julienned cucumbers, mung bean sprouts, and vegan fish dipping sauce.

CLEAR MUNG BEAN DUMPLINGS

Originating in Central Vietnam, this dish features savory mung beans encased in a translucent, chewy dumpling. Most dumpling shops in Vietnam only offer this dish twice a month: on the days of the full and new moons, which is when most Vietnamese Buddhists eat vegetarian dishes (ăn chay).

SKILL LEVEL Advanced | **YIELD** 30 to 40 dumplings

FILLING

3 tablespoons vegetable oil

1 ounce (28 g) shallot or leek, minced

½ cup (100 g) mashed mung beans (page 11)

1 tablespoon sugar

1 teaspoon vegetable or mushroom stock powder

½ teaspoon salt

DOUGH

3 cups (390 g) tapioca starch, divided

1 cup plus 2 teaspoons (250 ml) boiling water

FOR SERVING

¼ cup (60 ml) scallion oil (page 26)

1 ounce (28 g) cilantro, roughly chopped

½ cup (42 g) croutons

½ cup (120 ml) vegan fish dipping sauce (page 20)

1. MAKE THE FILLING In a medium skillet, heat oil over medium-low heat. When hot, add the shallot and cook and stir until fragrant (about 1 minute). Add mashed mung beans and stir for 1 minute. Add sugar, stock powder, and salt, and keep stirring until mixture comes together in a solid mass (about 2 minutes). Remove from heat and set aside to cool.

2. Take about ½ tablespoon of the filling, shape into a small ball, and repeat until you've used it all.

3. MAKE THE DOUGH Put 2 cups (260 g) of the tapioca starch in a medium bowl and set aside. In another medium bowl, combine the remaining 1 cup (130 g) tapioca starch and boiling water, and stir briskly with a wooden spoon until starch is translucent. Let cool for about 30 seconds, and then, using a rubber spatula, scrape the sticky paste into the other bowl that contains the tapioca starch and mix well.

4. Knead with your hands until you have a nice smooth dough (about 5 minutes). Cover bowl with a towel or plastic wrap and set aside

5. Pinch off a small portion of dough (about 1 tablespoon) and roll between your palms to shape into a ball. Press with your fingers to flatten it into a disc about 2½ inches (6 cm) in diameter. Try to avoid making your dumplings too large, as they will then be too chewy and difficult to swallow.

6. Place a filling ball in the center of each disc, and then fold it in half. Pinch the edges together to form a crescent-moon shape. Repeat with remaining dough and filling.

7. Fill a large saucepan halfway with water and bring to a boil. Gently drop in dumplings and cook them over low heat until they float to the surface (about 5 minutes). Remove from heat, cover, and let sit for 2 minutes. Prepare a large bowl of ice water. When the edges of the dumplings turn translucent (you should be able to see the yellow filling inside at this point), transfer them with a slotted spoon to the bowl of ice water.

8. FOR SERVING Toss the boiled dumplings in the scallion oil, sprinkle with cilantro and croutons, and serve with vegan fish dipping sauce.

🌿 **NOTE** *To freeze these dumplings, prepare but don't cook them. Spread them out on a dry surface, let sit for 30 minutes, and then put them in an airtight bag. They will keep for up to 6 months. Don't defrost them before cooking.*

STICKY RICE DUMPLINGS WITH COCONUT FILLING

These dumplings (bánh ít) are often presented on special occasions, such as anniversaries or the New Year. They can be savory or sweet and made with or without banana leaf. In this recipe, you will create a coconut filling, which is more popular in Southern Vietnam.

SKILL LEVEL Advanced | **YIELD** 10 dumplings

DOUGH AND WRAPPERS

2 cups (250 g) glutinous rice (or sticky rice) flour

1 teaspoon salt

2 tablespoons granulated sugar

1 cup (240 ml) warm water (176°F/80°C)

2 tablespoons vegetable oil, for greasing hands

10 pieces (8 by 8 inches/20 by 20 cm) banana leaves, prepped (page 15) (see Note)

FILLING

1 tablespoon vegetable oil

1½ cups (150 g) shredded young coconut or ¾ cup (75 g) dried coconut flakes

¼ teaspoon salt

3 tablespoons brown sugar

¼ cup (36 g) crushed roasted peanuts

2 tablespoons roasted sesame seeds

1. MAKE THE DOUGH In a large bowl, combine flour, 1 teaspoon of salt, and granulated sugar. Add warm water slowly, a little bit at a time (you might need a bit more or less than 1 cup/240 ml, depending on the ambient humidity). Knead with your hand until a nice smooth dough forms. Cover dough with plastic wrap and let rest for 30 minutes.

2. MAKE THE FILLING Heat 1 tablespoon of vegetable oil in a medium skillet over low heat. When hot, add coconut, ¼ teaspoon of salt, and brown sugar, and stir constantly until sugar melts and coconut becomes sticky (if you use dried coconut flakes, add a few tablespoons of water). Turn off heat and let cool. Combine with crushed peanuts and roasted sesame seeds, and then divide into 10 equal-size portions.

3. ASSEMBLE Grease your hands with some vegetable oil and divide dough into 10 equal-size portions. Roll each portion into a ball, and then flatten into ½-inch (1 cm) thick discs. Place one portion of filling in the center, gather the edges, and pinch to seal. Roll it between your palms to shape into a ball.

4. Place a banana-leaf square on a flat surface, darker, shiny side facedown, and fold in half to form a wide triangle. Lift up one of the far corners and roll it into the center until the edge is touching the middle of the triangle. With your other hand, bring in the other corner and roll it over top so it wraps around the other corner and shapes it into a cone. Drop the dough ball into it, and then fold in the four sides, creating a pyramid-shaped dumpling. Repeat with remaining dough, filling, and banana leaves.

5. Fill a steamer halfway with water and arrange the dumplings in the basket. Wrap the steamer lid in a towel and tie the corners over the handle. This will absorb some of the excess steam. Bring the water to a boil over high heat, cover, and steam over medium heat until all traces of white flour have disappeared, and the dough is slightly green (15 to 20 minutes). Remove from heat and allow to cool before unwrapping and enjoying.

NOTE *If you don't have banana leaves, place each dough ball from step 3 on a 2-inch (5 cm) square of parchment paper, leaving enough space between them in the steamer to avoid sticking, and then steam them.*

CRÊPES WITH MUSHROOMS

These popular crêpes are commonly made with rice flour colored with turmeric to get their distinctive appearance. The batter is spread evenly across a piping hot pan to create that sizzling sound, hence the name bánh xèo (which means "sizzling cake").

SKILL LEVEL Moderate | **YIELD** 16 crêpes

CRÊPES

3 cups (400 g) rice flour

⅓ teaspoon turmeric powder

½ teaspoon salt

3 cups (760 ml) water

1 ounce (28 g) scallion or leek (green part only), finely chopped

FILLING

2 pounds (907 g) assorted mushrooms (button, king oyster, beech, straw, shiitake, or oyster), stems trimmed

2 cups (480 ml) plus 2 tablespoons vegetable oil, divided

1 tablespoon minced scallion or leek (white part only)

½ teaspoon salt

1 teaspoon vegetable or mushroom stock powder

1 tablespoon vegan fish sauce (page 20) or soy sauce

1 pound (454 g) mung bean sprouts

FOR SERVING

1 pound (454 g) mustard greens (page 16) or leaf lettuce

3½ ounces (100 g) fresh green herbs (mint, perilla, cilantro, and/or Asian basil leaves), chopped

1 medium cucumber, peeled, seeds removed, and cut lengthwise into 3-inch (7.5 cm) slices

1 medium green mango, peeled, seeds removed, and cut lengthwise into 3-inch (7.5 cm) slices

1½ cups (320 ml) vegan fish dipping sauce (page 20)

1. MAKE THE CRÊPES In a large bowl, whisk rice flour, turmeric powder, salt, and water until well combined and batter is quite thin. Stir in finely chopped scallion and let sit for 30 minutes.

2. MAKE THE FILLING Cut larger mushrooms into ½-inch (1 cm) thick slices and separate smaller ones into bite-size bundles. Rinse well and squeeze out excess water.

3. Heat 2 tablespoons of the vegetable oil in a medium pan over medium-low heat. Add minced scallion and cook and stir until slightly golden brown (about 1 minute). Add mushrooms and season with salt, stock powder, and vegan fish sauce. Cook and stir until the mushrooms are wilted (about 3 minutes), and then remove pan from the heat.

4. Place an 8-inch (20 cm) cast-iron or heavy-bottomed skillet over medium heat. When hot, add 2 tablespoons of vegetable oil and swirl to evenly coat the pan. When oil starts to smoke, ladle ¼ cup (60 ml) of batter into the pan. It will start to sizzle immediately, so swirl the pan gently until mixture evenly covers the entire bottom. Spoon about ½ cup (35 g) of the cooked mushrooms and 1 ounce (28 g) of mung bean sprouts into the center of the crêpe, and then cover. When crêpe turns crispy and golden (about 3 minutes), use a heatproof spatula to fold it in half (see Note), and then continue to cook for 30 more seconds. Use a spatula to carefully transfer to a cooling rack to drain. Repeat with remaining vegetable oil, batter, mushroom filling, and mung bean sprouts.

5. FOR SERVING Cut the crêpes in half with kitchen scissors and place each half in the center of a leaf of mustard greens or lettuce. Top with the fresh green herbs, cucumber and green mango slices, and then roll it up. Serve with vegan fish dipping sauce.

NOTE *Be sure that you don't rush the folding part of the crêpe. It's always best to wait for one side of the crêpe to turn golden brown and crispy (watch the edges). The crêpe will then release itself from the pan and you will be able to lift and fold it with very little effort.*

DESSERTS & SNACKS

Whether you are in the mood for something sweet, salty, or a little bit of both, this section has it all! Need a tantalizing dessert to serve at a dinner party or take to a potluck? You can't go wrong with a classic like grilled bananas wrapped in sticky rice or steamed taro cake. Need a crispy snack to enjoy while binge-watching your favorite show? Whip up a batch of crispy macaroni or roasted garlic chili peanuts—you may never settle for plain old popcorn again.

THREE-COLOR STICKY RICE

This dessert (xôi ba màu) features a red layer of gấc sticky rice, a yellow layer of mashed mung beans, and a green layer of pandan sticky rice. Gấc fruit is native to Vietnam and is also called cochinchin gourd, Momordica charantia fruit, or baby jackfruit. You will need sticky rice molds (6 inches/15 cm) to make this dish, which you can purchase online or at most Asian grocery stores.

SKILL LEVEL Advanced | **YIELD** 8 servings

GREEN STICKY RICE

10 pandan leaves, finely chopped

1 cup (240 ml) water

1¼ cups (250 g) sticky rice, rinsed, soaked for 4 to 8 hours, and drained

RED STICKY RICE

3½ ounces (100 g) gấc fruit seeds with aril or 2 ounces (56 g) gấc fruit paste (see Note)

1 tablespoon white Chinese rice cooking wine (optional)

1¼ cups (250 g) sticky rice, rinsed, soaked for 4 to 8 hours, and drained

½ teaspoon salt

1 cup (240 ml) full-fat, unsweetened coconut milk

Pinch of salt

¼ cup (50 g) sugar

YELLOW LAYER

1 recipe mashed mung beans (page 11 make them with an additional ¼ cup/50 g peeled split mung beans and an additional ¼ cup/60 ml water)

2 tablespoons sugar

1. MAKE THE GREEN STICKY RICE In a blender, combine the chopped pandan leaves and water and pulse until smooth. Soak sticky rice in pandan juice for 4 to 6 hours. Drain in a colander, shake off excess water, and set aside.

2. MAKE THE RED STICKY RICE In a large bowl, combine gấc seeds with aril or gấc paste and cooking wine (if using). Wearing plastic gloves, mix vigorously to remove pulps and arils from the stones, then discard the stones (skip this last part if you used the paste). Add soaked rice and salt to the bowl and toss well until coated red.

3. Fill a large pot that can hold an 8- to 10-inch (20 to 25 cm) steamer basket with water until it is 1 inch (2.5 cm) below the base of the basket, and bring to a boil over medium-high heat. Line steamer basket with a banana leaf or piece of parchment paper to prevent rice from falling through the grates and sticking. Spread the red and green rice evenly, side by side in the steamer basket, and then poke a few holes through the layer. Wrap the steamer lid in a kitchen towel and tie the corners over the handle to absorb excess steam and prevent it dropping in the rice. Cover the steamer basket and place it on top of the boiling pot. Steam until the rice is tender, sticky, slightly chewy, and no longer opaque (35 to 40 minutes).

4. In a small bowl, mix coconut milk, salt, and ¼ cup (50 g) of sugar. Stir to dissolve. During the last 15 minutes of steaming, drizzle one-third of the coconut milk mixture over the rice. Cover and steam for 5 minutes. Repeat three more times until all the coconut milk mixture is gone.

5. MAKE THE YELLOW LAYER In a medium bowl, mix mashed mung beans with 2 tablespoons of sugar until combined.

6. ASSEMBLE Place a sticky rice mold on a flat surface with the patterned side facedown. Fill the mold one-third full with red or green sticky rice and spread in an even layer. Continue with a similar amount of mashed mung beans, and then another layer of the remaining color of sticky rice. Compress with the lid of the mold to form into a sticky rice cake, and then immediately unmold to reveal the beauty of three-color sticky rice.

 NOTE *You can find frozen gấc seeds with aril in packets. The red pulp is also sold in plastic cans labeled as frozen baby jackfruit paste at most Asian grocery stores. Alternatively, follow the steps for green sticky rice and replace pandan juice with beet juice to make the red sticky rice.*

GRILLED BANANAS WRAPPED IN STICKY RICE

I used to ride my bike home from school, and whenever I passed a street vendor selling chuối bọc nếp nướng, I simply couldn't resist the tempting aroma—neither will you.

SKILL LEVEL Advanced | **YIELD** 4 servings

BANANAS AND STICKY RICE

4 ripe Asian dwarf bananas, peeled

2 tablespoons sugar, divided

1 cup (200 g) sticky rice, rinsed, soaked for 1 hour, and drained

Pinch of salt

¼ cup (60 ml) water

¼ cup (60 ml) full-fat, unsweetened coconut milk

2 pandan leaves, knotted into a set, or 1 teaspoon vanilla extract

Vegetable oil, for greasing hands (optional)

4 pieces (2 by 6 inches/5 by 15 cm) and 4 pieces (3 by 6 inches/7.5 by 15 cm) banana leaves, prepped (page 15)

SAUCE

1 cup (240 ml) full-fat, unsweetened coconut milk

1 tablespoon sugar

½ teaspoon tapioca starch or cornstarch

2 pandan leaves, knotted into a set, or 1 teaspoon vanilla extract

3 tablespoons crushed roasted peanuts, for garnish (optional)

1. MAKE THE BANANAS AND STICKY RICE Place bananas in a medium bowl and toss with 1 tablespoon of the sugar. Cover and refrigerate for about 30 minutes.

2. Toss the sticky rice with the pinch of salt, then add to a small saucepan with a tight-fitting lid with the water and ¼ cup (60 ml) of coconut milk. Add 1 set of the knotted pandan leaves and bring to a boil. Cook uncovered over medium heat, stirring occasionally, until water level drops below the surface of the rice (about 5 minutes). Reduce heat to low, cover, and cook for an additional 15 minutes. Remove from heat and let sit for 5 minutes.

3. Remove and discard pandan leaves, add the remaining 1 tablespoon sugar and fluff with a fork or pair of chopsticks. While rice is still warm, wear gloves or grease your hands and pinch one-quarter of the rice and squeeze to compress it into a single solid mass. Spread a 12-inch (30 cm) square piece of plastic wrap on a flat surface and place the sticky rice mass on it, slightly off-center. Fold the plastic wrap in half to cover the rice. Use a rolling pin to flatten it into a ⅔-inch (1.7 cm) thick oval disc.

4. Unfold the plastic wrap and place a banana in the center on top of the rice. With the plastic wrap, fold the rice over to fully cover the banana, making sure the rice encloses and adheres to it tightly. Twist the ends of the plastic wrap tightly like a piece of taffy. Remove the plastic wrap and use a smaller piece of banana leaf to wrap around the banana lengthwise and a larger piece to wrap around the width. Repeat with the remaining bananas, sticky rice, and banana leaves.

5. Grill the four parcels, uncovered, on a charcoal or gas grill (uncovered) or in an infrared stove at 480°F (250°C), rotating occasionally. When the banana leaves are scorched and the surface of the sticky rice is dry to the touch (after about 10 minutes), you can remove both leaves. Continue to grill, rotating occasionally, until a crispy golden crust forms (about 15 more minutes).

6. MAKE THE SAUCE In a small saucepan, combine 1 cup (240 ml) of coconut milk, 1 tablespoon of sugar, tapioca starch, and knotted pandan leaves, and whisk well. Bring to a boil over medium-high heat, whisking constantly, until slightly thickened (about 3 minutes). Remove and discard pandan leaves.

7. Cut rolls into bite-size pieces, drizzle with sauce, sprinkle on crushed roasted peanuts (if using), and serve hot.

GREEN STICKY RICE WITH COCONUT

Fresh green sticky rice (cốm) is harvested mostly in autumn, so if you visit Hanoi during that time, it's a must-try! Green rice is immature rice that has been roasted and ground with a mortar and pestle until it's flat to create flakes. Cốm can be eaten raw with a banana (you just dip the fruit in it) or cooked in various dishes. This recipe (cốm xào dừa) is one of the simplest ways to enjoy green sticky rice: stir-fried with some shredded coconut. In Vietnam, this dish is often served on a sheet of crispy foam-like rice cracker (bánh tráng giấy gói xôi), so it's more convenient to hold and eat. However, as these are hard to find outside of Vietnam, you can substitute any other kind of rice cracker to get the same contrast in texture.

SKILL LEVEL Basic | **YIELD** 4 servings

1 cup (128 g) dried green sticky rice flakes (see Note)

½ cup (120 ml) full-fat, unsweetened coconut milk

2 ounces (56 g) shredded young coconut or 1 ounce (28 g) dried coconut flakes, rehydrated (see Note)

2 tablespoons sugar

4 rice crackers, for serving

2 teaspoons (8 g) toasted sesame seeds, for garnish

1. In a medium bowl, combine dried green sticky rice with coconut milk, mix well, and let sit for 10 minutes.

2. In a medium skillet, combine shredded coconut and sugar, and cook over medium-low heat, stirring constantly, for about 2 minutes.

3. Add rice and cook and stir until all rice flakes come together to make one sticky gelatinous mass (3 to 5 minutes). Remove from heat.

4. Divide the mixture into 4 equal-size portions and spoon each onto the center of a rice cracker. Sprinkle with sesame seeds and serve.

🌱 **NOTE** *Outside Vietnam, dried green sticky rice flakes (also called green rice flakes) are sold in packets online or at most Asian grocery stores. You should also be able to find shredded young coconut in the frozen section for the topping. Alternatively, you can buy dried coconut flakes anywhere, and then just soak them in an equal amount of coconut milk to rehydrate them.*

STEAMED TARO CAKE

This yummy dessert (bánh khoai môn hấp) is from the southwest region of Vietnam. As taro has purple-tinged flesh, most dishes created or flavored with it feature its signature color. However, because the ratio of taro to flour in this cake is rather low, you will use purple cabbage as a natural coloring agent.

SKILL LEVEL Moderate | **YIELD** 8 servings

¼ small purple cabbage, rinsed and shredded

1½ cups (360 ml) water, divided

1 cup (150 g) rice flour

6 tablespoons tapioca starch

½ cup (100 g) sugar

1 cup (240 ml) full-fat, unsweetened coconut milk

Pinch of salt

1 tablespoon vanilla extract

1 pound (454 g) taro (page 17), peeled and thinly sliced

1 teaspoon vegetable oil

1. Combine shredded cabbage with 1 cup (240 ml) of the water in a medium bowl, and let sit for 15 minutes.

2. Drain through a sieve into a large bowl and discard shredded leaves (or save for salads). Add rice flour, tapioca starch, sugar, coconut milk, salt, vanilla extract, and the remaining ½ cup water, and stir until smooth.

3. Separate taro slices and drop them into the batter.

4. Lightly grease an 8-inch (20 cm) round silicone or aluminum baking pan with oil. Pour batter into pan and even out until it covers the bottom.

5. Fill a steamer halfway with water and place baking pan in the basket. Wrap the steamer lid in a large kitchen towel and tie the corners of the fabric over the handle. This will absorb the excess steam and prevent it from dropping back down on the cake. Bring the water to a boil, cover, and steam until a chopstick inserted in the center comes out clean (35 to 40 minutes). Remove from steamer and let cool completely.

6. Run a knife along the edges of the pan to loosen and unmold the cake. Transfer to a platter or cake stand lined with parchment paper or banana leaf to prevent sticking. With a lightly oiled knife, cut the cake into 8 equal portions and serve.

CRISPY BANANA SPRING ROLLS

Banana spring rolls (chả giò chuối) are a simple dessert that you can whip up in no time at all. The hint of cinnamon also makes them the perfect snack for a cold winter day. For the wrappers, it's best to use those that are labeled for "spring roll pastries" (the Spring Home brand is probably the most popular) or lumpia wrappers (such as the Simex brand).

SKILL LEVEL Basic | **YIELD** 16 rolls

2½ tablespoons light or dark brown sugar

½ tablespoon ground cinnamon

4 ripe Asian dwarf bananas, cut lengthwise into 4 sticks, or 2 Cavendish bananas, cut into 4-inch (10 cm) lengths and then quartered lengthwise

16 square spring roll pastry wrappers (7½ inches/19 cm) (page 11)

2 cups (480 ml) vegetable oil, for deep-frying

¼ cup (60 ml) vegan chocolate syrup, for serving (optional)

¼ cup (28 g) powdered sugar, for serving (optional)

1. On a rimmed plate, combine brown sugar and cinnamon and mix well. Roll one piece of banana in the mixture and place on a wrapper, closer to one corner. Fold the sides of the wrapper over to cover the ends of the banana, and then lift up the corner with the banana and roll tightly until reaching the opposite corner to encase the filling. Using a pastry brush or your finger, brush the exposed edge of the wrapper with a bit of water, and then tightly roll the cylinder up to the end of the wrapper to seal it. Place the spring roll, seam side down, on a plate. Repeat with remaining banana pieces and wrappers.

2. Fill the bottom of a medium saucepan with about 2 inches (5 cm) of oil and heat over medium heat. When oil reaches 320°F (160°C) on a cooking thermometer, gently drop in a few rolls. (You can also dip the pointy end of a wooden chopstick into the oil; if a steady stream of tiny bubbles appears around it, it's ready.) Fry the rolls in batches to avoid overcrowding the pan until golden brown on all sides (3 to 5 minutes), and then transfer with a wire spider or slotted spoon to a cooling rack or paper towel–lined plate to drain.

3. Drizzle with chocolate syrup (if using) and dust with the powdered sugar (if using), and serve warm.

BANANA CAKE WITH RAISINS

If you're having some friends over and want to treat them to a sweet, delicious dessert, baked banana cake with raisins (bánh chuôì nướng nho khô) is a fantastic choice! While this cake is a bit time consuming, it's not that difficult to make—just be sure to read through the recipe a few days before your event so you can plan ahead.

SKILL LEVEL Moderate | **YIELD** 8 servings

2 pounds (907 g) ripe Asian dwarf bananas, thinly sliced

3 tablespoons red wine or rum

¼ cup (50 g) sugar

1 tablespoon vegan butter or margarine

1 can (13½ ounces/400 ml) full-fat, unsweetened coconut milk

3½ ounces (100 g) unsweetened vegan yogurt

⅓ cup (50 g) rice flour

5 slices (7 ounces/200 g) day-old sandwich bread or baguette, torn into small pieces

⅔ cup (100 g) raisins, divided

1. In a large bowl, combine bananas, red wine, and sugar, and toss gently. Cover and leave to marinate overnight in the refrigerator.

2. Place banana-wine mixture in a large skillet and bring to a boil over medium heat. Reduce heat to low and simmer, occasionally stirring, until the liquid is slightly thickened (8 to 10 minutes).

3. Preheat oven to 350°F (175°C). Lightly grease bottom and sides of an 8-inch (20 cm) baking pan with vegan butter, and then line with parchment paper.

4. In a large bowl, whisk coconut milk, yogurt, and rice flour together until smooth. Stir in bread pieces, and then (while wearing gloves) squeeze the pieces to soften them and help them absorb the liquid. Add two-thirds of the simmered banana slices and three-quarters of the raisins, and stir well.

5. Pour the mixture into the prepared baking pan and smooth the surface with a spatula. Arrange the remaining simmered banana slices and raisins on top.

6. Cover the pan with aluminum foil, bake for 45 minutes, and then remove foil and bake for another 45 minutes. During the last 10 minutes of baking, check the cake. The bananas around the edges will caramelize faster, so to help the top brown evenly, cut a circle, 6 inches (15 cm) in diameter, in the center of the aluminum foil that is large enough to expose the uncaramelized surface to heat. Cover with the foil and continue to bake until the top of the cake is caramelized evenly.

7. Remove from the oven, allow to cool in the pan, and then refrigerate overnight before serving. This allows the cake to set firmly and the flavors to deepen.

8. Before serving, remove the cake from the baking pan and cut into slices. Serve cold.

CRISPY MACARONI

If you ask me which Vietnamese snack is most similar to chips (think Pringles or Doritos), I would say nui chiên! It's just the thing to satisfy those between-meal cravings. Rice macaroni is deep-fried and then tossed with savory seasonings. I recommend using elbow macaroni or corkscrew- or spiral-shaped pasta, like fusilli, for the ultimate crispy puffiness. However, note that you must use macaroni or pasta made with white or brown rice flour for this recipe, as traditional Italian pastas are made from wheat flour and become hard when fried. You'll want to serve these within 2 hours after cooking or keep them in an airtight container. If left out for too long, the macaroni will lose its crispness.

SKILL LEVEL Basic | **YIELD** 2 servings

1 cup (240 ml) vegetable oil

2 ounces (56 g) rice elbow macaroni or other twisty pasta (such as fusilli, rotini, cavatappi, or pipe rigate)

1 tablespoon vegan butter or margarine

2 cloves garlic, minced

1 teaspoon vegan fish sauce (page 20)

1 tablespoon sugar

1 tablespoon water

½ teaspoon chili flakes

1. In a small saucepan, heat vegetable oil over medium heat until hot (about 3 minutes). To test, stick one end of a chopstick in the oil; if bubbles appear around it, it's ready.

2. Drop in the macaroni. They tend to pop up and brown fast (within a few seconds); when they do, use a slotted spoon to transfer quickly to a paper towel–lined plate to drain.

3. In a small pan melt the vegan butter and cook and stir the garlic over medium-low heat until slightly golden (about 30 seconds). Add the vegan fish sauce, sugar, and water, and simmer until sugar is dissolved and sauce has thickened slightly (about 1 minute).

4. Add the crispy macaroni and toss until coated with sauce (about 30 seconds). Remove from heat, sprinkle with chili flakes, and enjoy immediately.

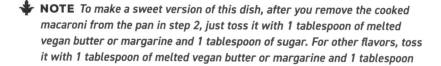 **NOTE** *To make a sweet version of this dish, after you remove the cooked macaroni from the pan in step 2, just toss it with 1 tablespoon of melted vegan butter or margarine and 1 tablespoon of sugar. For other flavors, toss it with 1 tablespoon of melted vegan butter or margarine and 1 tablespoon of vegan cheese powder or 1 teaspoon of cocoa or matcha powder.*

ROASTED GARLIC CHILI PEANUTS

Roasted garlic chili peanuts (đậu phộng rang tỏi ớt) are a popular crunchy snack in both Central and South Vietnam. They go well with beer, but you can also serve them as a side dish with rice or porridge. Heating the peanuts with salt helps ensure they're all roasted evenly.

SKILL LEVEL Moderate | **YIELD** 6 servings

1 cup (175 g) raw peanuts with skins, rinsed and drained

2½ teaspoons salt, divided

¼ cup (60 ml) vegetable oil

1 head garlic, minced

2 bird's eye chili peppers, minced

1 teaspoon plus 1 tablespoon sugar, divided

¼ cup (60 ml) water

½ tablespoon all-purpose flour

½ tablespoon cornstarch

1. Place peanuts and 2 teaspoons of the salt in a medium saucepan or wok and heat over medium heat, stirring constantly, until the skins begin to crack and loosen (10 to 15 minutes). Remove from heat. Immediately transfer peanuts to a fine-mesh sieve and shake it well to eliminate all the salt. Set aside.

2. In a clean, medium skillet, heat oil over medium-low heat. When hot, add garlic and chili peppers and cook and stir until slightly golden (30 to 45 seconds). With a slotted spoon, transfer fried garlic and chili peppers to a small bowl, leaving oil in the pan. Stir in the remaining ½ teaspoon salt and 1 teaspoon of the sugar, and then set aside.

3. In a small bowl, combine the remaining 1 tablespoon sugar and the water. Stir until sugar is dissolved and set aside.

4. Remove half of garlic oil from skillet, and then heat remaining oil in pan over medium-low heat. Add roasted peanuts and sift in flour. Stir constantly until peanuts are coated with flour (about 1 minute). Sift in cornstarch and stir constantly until peanuts are coated with it (about 1 more minute). Pour in sugar-water mixture and stir constantly for 30 seconds. Add fried garlic-chili mixture and toss well over low heat until peanuts are thoroughly coated with the sticky syrup and garlic-chili mixture (about 1 more minute).

5. Remove from heat, spread peanuts on a baking sheet, and allow to cool completely.

6. After the peanuts have cooled, store in a jar or airtight container and refrigerate for up to 1 month.

SPICY CASSAVA FRITTERS

Cassava (yuca) is a starchy tuberous root that is a staple ingredient in many Latin and Caribbean dishes. It is also used in many dishes in certain parts of Asia, including Indonesia, Thailand, and Vietnam. These spicy fritters (bánh cay) are the perfect finger food to serve at a party or to enjoy as a snack. They're crispy on the outside and glutinous and chewy on the inside. You can usually find frozen grated cassava at an Asian grocery store, but if you prefer, you can prepare it yourself. Cassava can be poisonous in its raw form, so you must always be sure to prep and cook it thoroughly before serving. First, cut off the tapered ends and divide the root into manageable lengths. Peel off the skin, and then quarter lengthwise and remove the woody cordon that runs along the root's axis. Soak the white flesh in water for 6 to 8 hours, changing the water every 2 hours to remove any toxins. Drain and finely grate with a box grater or in a food processor until smooth.

SKILL LEVEL Moderate | **YIELD** 25 fritters

1 pound (454 g) cassava roots, peeled, soaked, and grated (see above), or frozen grated cassava, thawed

½ teaspoon salt

1 teaspoon sugar

1 to 2 teaspoons chili powder

2 tablespoons chopped scallion

2 tablespoons all-purpose flour (see Note)

2 cups (480 ml) vegetable oil, for deep-frying

1. In a large bowl, combine the grated cassava, salt, sugar, chili powder, scallion, and flour, and mix well.

2. Grab a pinch (about 1 tablespoon) of the paste and roll it between your palms to shape into an oval cocoon that is about 2 inches (5 cm) long and 1 inch (2.5 cm) thick in the middle. Repeat with remaining paste.

3. In a small saucepan or a wok, heat the oil over medium heat until it reaches 320°F (160°C) on a cooking thermometer. (You can also dip the pointy end of a wooden chopstick into the oil; if a steady stream of tiny bubbles appears around it, the oil is ready.)

4. Gently drop in the cassava cocoons and fry in batches, turning often, until golden brown (about 15 minutes). With a wire spider or slotted spoon, transfer fritters to a cooling rack or paper towel–lined plate to drain.

5. Serve within 1 hour after frying. You can store any leftovers in an airtight container and re-fry them whenever you are ready to serve.

 **NOTE** *You can replace the all-purpose flour with rice flour, tapioca starch, or cornstarch for a gluten-free option.*

INDEX

ACKNOWLEDGMENTS

I can't thank my followers enough for their trust in, and love for, my recipes. Their encouraging comments and feedback have been what urged me to continue doing what I do for the last decade.

It has been a pleasure to work with Erin Canning at Rock Point on both my previous book, *Simply Pho*, and this one. A thousand thanks to her for all of her consideration, negotiation, and guidance to bring this book to life.

My heartfelt thanks to Happy Le at Detas Studio for the professional food photos, Amanda Gambill for the excellent editing work, and Marisa Kwek and Lisa Berman for the spectacular design and layout of this book.

I would also like to thank Hoang Ngoc Anh Tho for helping me with the draft translation of this book and my team at *Helen's Recipes* for assisting me with the heavy workload of cookbook compiling and daily content creation.

I am so grateful to have my husband, Kevin, and two little angels, Phở and Mỳ (yes, I nicknamed them after my favorite noodles), who are always the biggest supporters of mommy's food. They are my ultimate motivation to work harder and be happier every day. I also send much love to my parents, Ngọc and Nhạn, for always believing in me and taking pride in my work.

ABOUT THE AUTHOR

Helen Le is the founder of one of the largest YouTube cooking channels on Vietnamese food with over 600,000 subscribers. She and her channel, *Helen's Recipes*, are often featured in the media as the (unofficial) ambassadors of Da Nang and Vietnamese cuisine.

In addition to publishing her own line of cookbooks internationally, Helen has also been recognized as one of the top four food influencers in Vietnam in the 2017 Influence Asia Awards, one of the top five finalists in the Seoul Fusion Hansik Cooking competition, a YouTube Ambassador in Vietnam, and the Culinary Ambassador for the Sheraton Grand Danang Resort. She has also appeared on numerous Vietnamese cooking programs, including *7-Minute Breakfasts, Home-Cooked Vietnam, and Home-Cooked Asia*.

For more information about Helen and her work, please visit her website at helenrecipes.com.